"Marco LeRoc's book is the ultime It explains everything from the cost of higher education to how to choose a college, obtain scholarships and successfully manage college debt. This book offers valuable information and offers real-life examples of how students can avoid huge college debts and graduate debt free. From my perspective as someone who funds college scholarships, Marco's book is spot on! The subjects covered in this book are timely, relevant, and very useful. I highly recommend this book."

—Scott Thompson, MBA, Author of *Art & Science of Value Investing: Invest Like Billionaire Warren Buffett*

"Tuition costs have skyrocketed since 2008—while the stock and job markets have plummeted. Colleges apparently didn't get the memo during the financial meltdown. Unemployment is directly related to level of education; and without a college degree, opportunities in the job market are dismal. What's a student to do? Marco LeRoc earned his college degree debt-free, and shares insight that is a must-read for all high school students and parents."

—J.P. Hansen, Award-Winning Author, *The Bliss List*

"Marco LeRoc has done it again. This Midwestern, no-nonsense money coach has broken down college debt into an easy-to-understand guide for parents and students alike. Marco separates himself from his peers by asking the question that students should ask themselves: What is the value of higher education for me? He asks students to take on an investor paradigm, and empowers them with a strategy to attain their goals while minimizing debt. This is a must-read for anyone who wants to invest in their future by investing in higher education."

—Brian Lambelet, Founder of Apparel Unlimited

"In *Screw College Debt*, Marco provides very pertinent information and OPTIONS! This book provides you with a 360-degree view of every path you can take to pursue your passion through any form of higher education, and do so in the most prepared, affordable, and financially responsible way!"

—Lamarr Womble, Founder of Passion for Leadership, Speaker, and Life Coach

"Marco LeRoc is passionate about helping people improve their personal financial management practices. Readers are enriched by reading his books, and by putting these thoughtful ideas into practice."

—Bud Labitan, MD, MBA, Author of *The Four Filters Invention of Warren Buffett and Charlie Munger* and *MOATS*

"The cost of attending college falls between purchasing a car and purchasing a house—all of us should put significant and structured thought into the decisions about attending, financing, and completing college. Marco LeRoc excels at raising awareness of the issues and offers specific suggestions about making the process work for you and your family."

—Dan Gilbert, Founder Learning Innovations, Inc.

"This book is a great resource for all future college students. The topics that Marco covers benefit applicants themselves and their parents. It informs them before they take that leap into higher education, and helps them to avoid college debt."

—Eric L. Ewing, Adjunct Professor, Bellevue University and Herzing University

"I wish this book had been available to me when I was pursuing my higher education. *Screw College Debt* provides tips on how to avoid college debts. The topic is both timely and relevant. It will inspire many students to make smart decisions when planning for college."

—Elizabeth Larson, MD

"*Screw College Debt* will help thousands of students not to major in debt."

—Charisse Conanan Johnson, CFA, Millennial Wealth Expert

"Great advice! This book serves as an insightful overview of the economics of higher education. Not only does it give an in-depth discussion on the history and current state of higher ed, it systematically breaks down the cycle of how students and families continuously fall into the debt trap and what this will mean for the US economy as a whole down the road. Two of the most important features of this book are the discussion about educational investment vehicles and tips for making college more affordable (including alternatives to the traditional college path). Parents and younger students should definitely utilize this information to start forming strategic plans surrounding education and career."

—Jamal Jackson, Speaker, Founder, and Managing Attorney, Jackson Corporate Law Offices, PC

"In his new book, *Screw College Debt: How to Go to College without Breaking the Bank*, Marco LeRoc provides simple, straightforward, and valuable information about getting through college without the crippling debt that so many college graduates face. From making astute cost comparisons (including not only tuition and fees, but also the cost of loans) to handling and minimizing all those peripheral costs (e.g., books, transportation, food, housing, entertainment), LeRoc presents commonsense tips for obtaining a high-quality education without high-level debt."

—Marian Shalander Kaiser, Writer, Author, and Professor at the University of Nebraska at Omaha

"Marco does it again! In this phenomenal follow-up to his *Cash In with Your Money*, he delivers the perfect guide for parents and students to navigate the world of college finance without breaking the bank and burying themselves in debt. As a journalist, I've covered countless stories of how to survive the ever-rising cost of higher education. Marco's wisdom is unmatched. This is the perfect gift for parents and students. And don't wait until high school graduation to get it. Read it now!"

—Efrem Graham, News Anchor and Correspondent,
Christian Broadcasting Network

"Marco LeRoc sums up the FACTS on college debt. Should I go to college? If so, where? How can I lessen my debt? Where can I apply for scholarships? This is THE resource for gaining the skills and knowledge you need to screw college debt."

—Katie Goergen, MD, Alumni, University of Iowa

"Simple, yet effective strategies for college students to manage and cope with student loan debt. *Screw College Debt* allows future students to truly live the American dream—debt-FREE. Concise and powerful!!!"

—Dina B., BS, Student, Creighton University

"A tremendously useful guide many students and parents need. In other words, this is a fine piece of art and a great book to start discussing well before high school graduation. Buying this book is certainly a smart investment in saving for college. I wish that I had it to rely on while I was going through college."

—Ayele E. Amavigan, EdD, MSW, President and Founder,
Hidden-Talent Foundation

"Face the reality: $1.2 trillion in total college debt is scary. At least, Marco cares enough to provide us with easy-to-follow tips on what it takes to avoid college debt. *Screw College Debt* is a must-read guide for anyone who wants to be successful in college and enjoy a debt-free life after graduation."

—Jeff Beals, Award-Winning Author, Professional Speaker, and
Former Dean of Students at Clarkson College

"I'm a recent college graduate, and after reading Marco's book, *Cash In with Your Money*, we knew we had to invite him to Stanford University to share some insights with students about how to manage their money. I'm excited to see that all of that wisdom has been put in book form with *Screw College Debt*. This is definitely the go-to for anyone who wants to reap the benefits of a college education while minimizing the huge financial burden!"

—Karl Kumodzi, Alumni, Stanford University

"Looking at the next 5 years, continual learning will be what makes the difference to your career, your livelihood and even your relationships—both personal and professional. Marco LeRoc not only teaches you how to increase your ability to pay for college, he prepares you to be a life-long learner. The days are over when parents would sacrifice their life savings, and student would take out loans that put them in massive debt upon graduation. As an 'untraditional' student myself (starting in a local city college, earning 2 Master's degrees, and going on to study at many universities), I appreciate the case that Marco makes for learning. This book will help you get to your next 'there.'"

—Jason W. Womack, MEd, MA - Executive Coach and
Author of *Your Best Just Got Better*

Also by Marco LeRoc

Cash In with Your Money: Tools for a Better Financial Life
ISBN: 978-0-9903612-1-3

SCREW COLLEGE DEBT

MARCO LEROC

SCREW COLLEGE DEBT

How to go to college without breaking the bank

MARCO LEROC

Ascendant
PRESS
www.AscendantPress.com

Copyright © 2015 Marco LeRoc

No part of this book may be used or reproduced in any manner whatsoever without written permission except in the case of brief quotations embodied in critical articles or reviews.

Because of the dynamic nature of the Internet, any Web addresses or links contained in this book may have changed since publication and may no longer be valid.

Any similarities to other intellectual works are either coincidental or have been properly cited when the source is known. Trademarks of products, services, and organizations mentioned herein belong to their respective owners and are not affiliated with the publisher, Ascendant Press.

Any people depicted in stock imagery provided by Thinkstock are models, and such images are being used for illustrative purposes only.

Paperback ISBN: 978-0-9903612-4-4
ePub ISBN: 978-0-9903612-6-8
Kindle ISBN: 978-0-9903612-5-1

Library of Congress Cataloging Number: 2015903791

Library of Congress data on file with the publisher.

Ascendant Press
PO Box 93
Omaha, NE 68010

www.MarcoLeRoc.com

Produced by Concierge Marketing Publishing Services,
www.conciergemarketing.com

Printed in the United States of America

10 9 8 7 6 5 4 3 2

To Isabela, Kendra, Brianna & Macie ....
What you need to know before heading to college

A note about websites: This book cites numerous web addresses. As of this writing, all are correct and working. In the world of the Internet, however, things change. Please be aware that some URLs may have changed since the author compiled these listings.

A note about financial information: The author has made an effort to ensure that the information in this book is accurate and up to date. Due to continually changing laws and regulations, however, some parts of the book may be outdated.

The information, ideas, and suggestions in this book are not intended to render professional advice. Before following any suggestion in this book, you should consult your personal accountant or other financial advisor. The examples in this book represent the opinions of the author and may not be applicable to all situations.

The author assumes no responsibility and disclaims all liabilities in connection with the use of this book. You should use caution in applying the material from this book, as it may not relate to your specific situation. You should always seek advice from a qualified professional.

Neither the author nor the publisher shall be liable or responsible for any loss or damage allegedly arising as a consequence of your use or application of any information or suggestion in this book.

The names of people associated with events described in this book were randomly chosen. Any similarity to actual people is coincidental.

Contents

Part VI: Managing College Debt

Part VII: College Savings Secrets

SCREW COLLEGE DEBT

MARCO LEROC

Introduction

Higher education in the United States is currently facing several significant challenges, not the least of which is the cost. At the same time that the need for a college education is rising, reductions in funding from state and local governments, tuition rate hikes, and the high cost of attending college are making it more difficult for students and their families to afford that education. As a result, more young people, and their parents, are taking out more student loans.

Student loan debts are soaring as high as flung mortarboards.

As of 2013, Americans owe over $1.2 trillion in student loan debts. According to the Federal Reserve Bank of New York, student loans are now the second largest source of personal debt behind a mortgage, surpassing credit cards and auto loans.

With an economy still recovering from the financial crisis of 2008, many graduates are having difficulty finding the type of employment that will allow them to make their student loan payments, leaving them with significant debt that they cannot afford to pay off. This has led to circumstances in which many graduates are defaulting on their loans, moving back with their parents, delaying major purchases, putting off starting a family and even changing their career choices, all of which has a negative impact on the economy.

Today we live in a society where higher education is vital for competing in the job market. The lack of quality higher education is a threat to our global competitiveness. But although higher education is needed, it is not a guarantee of success. The only guarantee is the hefty cost that comes with earning the degree.

The high cost of college, with no assurance of employment at the end, has led many students to wonder if student loans are no longer a good debt, as previously considered, but a bad debt, and if college is indeed worth it. The college debt crisis is looming as the next financial bubble, with the high rate of defaults threatening to be the instrument that bursts it.

Yet despite all these concerns, higher education is important and is of value. The question doesn't need to be, "Is college worth the cost?" The question should be, "What is the value of my college education?" Every college student should ask themselves this before taking out loans and heading to college.

Three years ago, I wrote my first book, *Cash In with Your Money: Tools for a Better Financial Life*. It was inspired by the financial crisis and one of its root causes: a lack of financial education.

Throughout that book, I shared information on how to become financially literate, get out of debt, save money and achieve the best financial results. I also founded Moneyvations LLC, which became Marco LeRoc & Companies, in order to inspire young adults to become successful financially and personally by developing the skills that they need to achieve their goals. As part of the work of that company, I travel frequently, speaking to audiences in the United States and abroad.

Many of my speaking engagements are at educational institutions—universities, colleges, and high schools. Discussions of student loans are occurring more and more frequently. I find that I enjoy engaging students on the topic of college debt. From the elite Stanford University on the West Coast, to Roosevelt University in the heart of downtown Chicago, to rural Concordia University in Seward, Nebraska, to Bentley University in Waltham, Massachusetts, I have had the privilege of interacting with many college students. A few are attending school with no debt because of great planning, but the majority are burdened. And beyond college, I have spoken to many young professionals with student loan yokes about their necks.

Like *Cash In with Your Money*, *Screw College Debt* raises awareness of the importance of financial literacy as it applies to college planning, and about being smart about handling—or completely avoiding—college debt.

Yes, tuitions are rising, and there are no federal government reforms to resolve the college debt crisis. But blaming and bemoaning these facts is not productive. It's up to students and their parents to be both proactive and creative in finding ways to fund college education.

Are You Another Frank?

In April 2012, I was traveling from Las Vegas, where I had attended the Hidden Talent Foundation board meeting, to Santa Cruz, California. It was a memorable flight. I've flown thousands of miles, but I was a Virgin America virgin, taking my first flight on British billionaire Richard Branson's airline.

Even more memorable was Frank. Frank was 22 and seated next to me. I introduced myself, and we chatted. He was returning to his hometown of San Mateo after losing his job working at a gallery. Frank was a dropout who had majored in women's studies. During our short flight Frank told me that he owed $142,000 in student loans, and this is why he dropped out: he didn't want any more debt. When I heard the amount, I thought it was an April Fool's joke. But it wasn't. I felt so bad for him, especially now being jobless. But he said he was more worried about his loans than his job situation. He recognized that he had made many mistakes, and he wished that he and his parents had planned and acted better before sending him off to college.

Screw College Debt is written to highlight the problems associated with the cost of higher education, including tuition fee hikes, the lack of college planning, and the demand for higher education.

There are millions of students struggling as a consequence of student loan debt. This book is for Frank and for all the Franks out there. But this book is also for high school graduates and prospective college students of all ages, so they may avoid excessive debt; for current college students, to help them avoid debt and save money while in school; for parents, so they can be aware of different investment options and can save for future college expenses; and for graduates (or parents of graduates) looking to learn about college debt repayment strategies.

The high cost of a college education, and the consequent problem of student debt, are bigger issues and are beyond the scope of this book. What I intend to do here is to provide strategies and resources so that students who choose to go to college can attend with less or no debt.

Students need to understand why they are heading to college, how student loans work, and the financial aid process.

Screw College Debt provides resources to help the college planning process, but most importantly, it offers ways to save for college and to avoid debt. I graduated debt-free; I went to a community college, worked and paid my way. Community colleges are economic ways to approach higher education. Parents can also start saving and investing when their children are young. From how to apply for scholarships, get cheaper loans, improve skills with Massive Open Online Courses, or save while in college, this book is a simple, complete, and practical guide to help you overcome or completely avoid college debt.

While I believe that higher education is necessary, I also believe that it isn't for everyone. But if you want it, you can have it, and without the shadow of debt. The bottom line is to find value in higher education without sacrificing or limiting the financial outlook for your future.

I hope *Screw College Debt* inspires and helps you save for college, enabling you to pursue higher education without accruing high levels of debt, so that the only thing you need to worry about after graduation is finding an apartment and a job. This book is your guide in the quest for obtaining a college degree with almost nothing, and graduating beholden to no one.

PART I | America's Higher Education Dilemma

1

Tuition Marathon

The cost of higher education is spiking out of control, making college education increasingly unaffordable. There are many explanations for the surge in college and university costs, but the latest financial crisis is primarily to blame.

The Impact of the Financial Crisis

Colleges and universities draw their revenues from tuitions, grants, state and local appropriations (for most public institutions), endowments, investment returns, private donations (for most private institutions), and revenue from other sources such as contracts, bookstores, dining halls, hospitals, and hotels.

When the financial crisis took its terrible toll on the US economy, it affected all of the revenue streams mentioned above. Years later those revenue streams are still recovering.

Public colleges and universities get their revenue from their state government. But the financial crisis forced many states to cut their budgets in response to falling tax revenues and an increased need for mandated services: emergency medical and low-income health providers, safety (police, fire), unemployment benefits, state-funded pensions. Since funding higher education is viewed as discretionary spending, public colleges and universities received significantly less from their local governments.

Private institutions were not immune to the impact of the financial crisis either. They lost money on their investments, contributions to endowments were low, and private donations were cut.

As a result, colleges and universities in both the public and private spheres raised tuitions to make up for the loss. Price hikes that continue to this day.

The average tuition at a four-year public college rose 15% between 2008 and 2010 in response to states cutting per-student funding to colleges. With an average cut of 13% between 2006 and 2011, states like South Carolina, Florida, California, Nevada, and Washington were most affected.

California, known for its higher education affordability, found itself in a financial mess with a deficit of hundreds of billions of dollars. With that amount of debt, the state was unable to provide the University of California system with its necessary funding. Consequently, in 2009 the UC system approved a plan to raise tuition 32% for the fall of 2010.

Historic Tuition Increases and Inflation

The recent financial crisis may have been the catalyst for a sharp upturn in tuition cost, but tuition rates have actually been climbing for many years.

An August 2012 Bloomberg publication revealed that college tuition and fees had surged 1,120% since 1978, four times faster than the increase in the consumer price index. A significant reason behind this was a gradual decline in state funding over that period.

Twenty years ago, tuition at the University of California, Los Angeles (UCLA) was $1,624; in 2012 it was $12,192. In 2000–2001, resident tuition and fees at the University of Nebraska at Lincoln were $3,522 per year; in 2011–2012 that amount had increased 115% to $7,563. A more dramatic surge occurred at the University of Kansas, which during the same period went from $2,725 to $9,222, a 238% increase.

In a short span of time, there have been myriad adjustments and spending shifts that have contributed to the rise of tuition prices:

- The cost of higher education has gone up more than inflation and adjusted inflation and is advancing far in excess of the inflation rate.

- According to the College Board, the average published tuition and fees at public four-year colleges and universities increased by 31% beyond the rate of inflation over the five years from 2002–2003 to 2007–2008, and by another 27% from 2007–2008 and 2012–2013.

- With its 1000% increase, tuition has outpaced the price of consumer goods, medical expenses, and food. Medical and food expenses rose respectively 601% and 244% .

- With an average increase of 8% a year, the cost of attending college effectively doubles every 10 years.

- A tuition cost estimated at $28,500, excluding room and board in 2012 at four-year private universities, could cost $58,000 or more today.

Tuitions and fees are on the rise, while median inflation-adjusted income is down over the past decade. It is increasingly difficult for parents and students to finance higher education, so they are borrowing more to pay for college. Consequently, the amount of college debt they amass is high and difficult to pay off. Many families have dipped into savings and retirement accounts to fund the cost of higher education, and others have taken out unsecured high-interest loans in lieu of the home equity loans often used in the past to fund education.

The Supply and Demand Issue

As a simple economic theory, we all know that when there is more demand for a product or a service, prices rise. Demand for higher education has been growing for quite some time.

There are historic reasons for this increase in demand, starting with increased accessibility. In 1862, President Abraham Lincoln signed the Morrill Act, granting federal land to the states to help them establish public colleges. Then in 1944, Congress passed the GI Bill to help World War II veterans further their education. Enrollment has been growing ever since.

In recent years, however, there has been a drastic rise in college enrollments. Four decades ago, enrollment at four-year institutions was around 5 million. By 2011 it had doubled to 10.6 million, but since then has nearly doubled again to 19 million today.

There are many reasons for this dramatic increase in enrollment.

A college degree is a gateway to success. Those with college degrees have a better chance to get a well-paying job and earn more over their lifetime compared to those without a college degree. Who doesn't want this success? So, each year, more and more students enroll and attend college, driving the price up.

Additionally, unemployment numbers rose during the recession. Many people who were laid off were advised to get loans and go to four-year institutions to qualify for better jobs. So mature students got loans and lived on them while studying. Enrollment rates shot up again as higher education became a refuge from the tumultuous job market.

The lack of available jobs didn't just affect those who were laid off. As the wars in Iraq and Afghanistan ended, many veterans returned home to find themselves with little or no job opportunities. They were trapped in a cycle of unemployment. They attended colleges and universities in the hope of bettering their prospects in the civilian sector, adding to the growing number of enrollments.

Then there is the influx of non-American students. Despite the problems in higher education, including rising tuitions, US colleges and universities continue to be huge draws for international students. Most of these students pay their tuition with private funds or scholarships. According to the Institute of International Education, the number of international students increased 5.7% from the year 2010–2011 to the year 2011–2012. The increasing number of international students is adding to the already growing number of US students, driving costs up even more.

Accessibility and availability are still a major concern to the public. Everyone wants a fair shot at earning a college degree. Due to the mounting demand for higher education, the government is forced to provide more subsidies, such as government loans, grants, and tax credits, in order to make college affordable. These subsidies make higher education available for certain incomes, fueling consumption and driving demand. For example, the number of recipients of Pell Grants (federal grants to low-income students) has increased significantly. In 1973–1974, there were 176,000 Pell Grant recipients. In 2001–2002, there were 3.8 million; and in 2010–2011, there were 8.9 million.

High demand equals scarcity of supplies. Colleges and universities can either meet the demand by increasing the supply or diminish the demand by raising prices. Increasing the supply means expansion—new buildings, faculty facilities—to accommodate the growing number of students, and, of course, someone has to foot that bill: the students.

Expansion also means expanding their pool of potential enrollees. Colleges and universities are now using extensive marketing campaigns to attract the best students (or just more students) to their campuses. They are hiring marketing professionals and spending thousands of dollars on TV and radio ads, publication in magazines and newspapers and billboard signs. These marketing campaigns are telling students what they want to hear, including that their college or university offers the best education, offers the most scholarships, provides more student services and amenities, and helps find or guarantees jobs for graduates.

As an example, the University of Southern California (USC), in one of its advertising campaigns in the *New York Times*, claimed that it gives more scholarships than any other institution. Yet the cost of publishing an ad in a major newspaper is probably equivalent to a scholarship itself!

The pursuit of students doesn't stop with ads. Recruiters lure prospective students into their facilities, especially targeting naïve high school students. Recruiters are rewarded according to how many students they enroll. They are salespersons for the benefit of their institutions and don't always represent the best interests of the students, working instead to meet target enrollment numbers set for them by the university.

Someone has to pay for these marketing expenses, and the costs are dumped on students through high tuitions.

Excessive Spending

To be competitive in attracting students, some colleges and universities are increasing their spending on student service facilities, such as by expanding their campuses, remodeling their existing infrastructures, or outfitting them with the latest in technological and residential amenities.

During the course of writing this book, I visited many colleges and universities, interviewing students and faculty. I was shocked by how fancy some of the institutions have become. State-of-the-art student halls, waterfalls, and expensive artwork—I could very well believe I was in a five-star hotel while visiting some schools. And while these upgrades are impressive, they are not intrinsic to quality education.

Colleges and universities of course have to expand to fit the needs of the growing student population. But ostentation is excessive and expensive; and despite a much-advertised influx of private donations or government money, the truth is that students absorb some or all of these costs.

Education Center vs. Sports Center

That brings us to another important question: are institutions with big-time sports activities good for students, or does the emphasis on athletics compromise the delivery of a high-quality education?

Some colleges are better known for their sports programs than for the caliber of the education they provide. This is especially true for schools with successful football and basketball teams. Prospective students are attracted to these schools because of their athletic achievements, not their academic reputation.

Colleges in the Big Ten Conference are well known; they have a steady stream of applicants and enrollments, but even they have to do whatever it takes to attract students away from their competitors. For the schools that have built their name on top of the success of their sports teams, this means maintaining or expanding their athletic facilities, and recruiting the best players and top-notch coaches, whatever the cost.

Significant spending at top athletic universities is driven by the desire to compete in college leagues rather than educational achievements. In his article, "Get Football Out of Our Universities," (*Forbes*, February 2011), Steven Salzberg expressed his disappointment in how many colleges and universities focus on football instead of education. According to Salzberg, in 2010, the University of Maryland, while furloughing faculty members and prohibiting even cost-of-living raises, paid $2 million to an outgoing coach in order to hire a new one.

Despite the lucrative, well-attended events at major sports schools, most of the athletic departments depend on subsidies derived from student fees and federal or state aid. According to *USA Today*, in 2012, just 23 of 228 athletic departments at NCAA Division I public schools generated enough money on their own to cover their expenses.

The Real Cost of Technology

We can't talk about the cause of tuition fee hikes without mentioning the costs associated with technology.

For some industries, the use of technology saves costs and lowers prices for consumers. This is not the case for higher education. Rather, technology is one of the reasons that tuition is rising. In this digital age, colleges and universities are forced to keep up with the ever-evolving technological trends. Online education and distance learning programs need to maintain and frequently update their technology in order to deliver a good service.

Colleges and universities spend a lot of money developing the right tools to teach effectively, do research, and connect with other faculty members and students. Students demand up-to-date applications and fast Internet connections that allow them to connect easily to social media; schools need media rooms, new computers, and touch-screen technology to attract them. A student recently told me she selected her university for its Apple computers and tablets over an institution with mere desktops.

To lure students and stay competitive, many colleges and universities go overboard with these "essential" toys and with the paychecks to the technicians and specialists who maintain them. On staff or by contract, these IT professionals are not cheap.

All this expense is, you guessed it, passed on to the students through their tuition.

Administrative and Faculty Expenses

As with all business—and institutions of higher education are businesses—universities employ thousands of people, for whom they provide healthcare, benefits, competitive salaries, and many other perks.

Employee wages and salaries are affected by inflation and the cost of living and are supplemented by healthcare, insurance, free or minimal tuition for themselves and their families, and retirement plans.

Good professors are valuable and can afford to be particular about where they will teach. In addition to their paycheck, pension, and healthcare, they need perks and incentives to come to any particular institution. Colleges and universities argue that these also drive tuition increases.

Universities claim that by paying their professors competitive salaries to retain them, they will be loyal and motivated to be productive; but what about the exorbitant salaries being paid to some university chancellors and presidents? When budgets are being cut and tuitions are being raised, how is it justified that university officials' salaries and compensation packages are being increased?

According to a survey by the *Chronicle of Higher Education*, the median total compensation for public university chancellors and presidents rose 3% from $409,483 in FY2010 to $421,395, during which time there were cuts at those same institutions.

In addition to their high salaries, top school officials also enjoy generous subsidies, bonuses, low-interest loans, and lavish residences at the expense of the college or university.

18

Another issue facing higher education is the increase in the number of administrative, nonacademic employees. The Goldwater Institute, a nonprofit public policy advocacy and research organization, found that between 1993 and 2007, the number of full-time administrators per 100 students at America's leading universities grew by 39%, while the number of employees engaged in teaching, research, or service grew by only 18%.

Why are higher education institutions engaging in a spending spree at the expense of state funds, grants, and rising tuitions? Why are colleges spending millions to house its officials while that money can be used to reduce tuition or provide affordable education?

Adding to the problem, there are issues of mismanagement at some higher education institutions. The ballooning payrolls and perks for top faculty and administrators are not the only mismanagement issues at colleges. Financial audits have found institutions mismanaging student financial aid, inaccurately reporting enrollment, creating fake vendors or giving contracts to friends or families, violating the institution's policies. The University of South Florida Polytechnic made the news for complaints of financial mismanagement at their Lakeland campus. The university was accused of laundering state education funds for unauthorized perks, using state money to purchase thousands of dollars in household appliances, hiring the son of a former university executive for a position in a university program for which he was unqualified (with a salary of over $50,000/year), and then giving the same executive's other son a $3,000 fee as a social media consultant.

This kind of egregious mismanagement and misappropriation is not common, but it does happen. And when it does, it helps further the spike in the exorbitant cost of pursuing higher education.

2

Lack of College Planning

Planning for college isn't an easy task and can be a daunting experience for those who don't have the knowledge to make the right decisions. Students and their parents need to avoid making costly financial decisions that will affect them not only in the short term, but also for a very long time.

The college application and enrollment process is complicated enough without tackling the issue of financing. Getting through the application process, deciding on housing, picking a major, completing the financial aid application, and sorting through different types of loans and repayment options are only the beginning. Students and parents have to fully understand the financial aid package they are signing themselves into.

Unfortunately, and despite the popularity of financial plan providers, many families still don't plan for college and are unprepared to fund the continuously growing cost of higher education. The reason for this can stem from several different issues.

Lack of Knowledge

One of the big hurdles facing families trying to fund a college education is that they lack the knowledge of the actual cost of that education.

Because of grants, scholarships, and financial aid packages, many students pay only a portion of the full college tuition. Despite these subsidies, however, what remains to be paid is still high and most of the time unaffordable; so most people end up taking out loans.

Tuition is not a constant—it increases almost every year, making college more expensive than what most people anticipate. For decades, tuition and fees at American four-year colleges and universities have risen at an annual rate of almost 8%.

But tuition is only a portion of the expenses, and many families don't anticipate the actual costs of housing, meal plans, transportation, books, student fees, entertainment, and other expenses. Not every student will be able to afford every school that accepts him or her, so when selecting a college, it is important to find out the actual entire cost of attending that school.

Students and parents choose colleges for a variety of reasons, sometimes for the bad ones. A student may prefer a certain school because his friends are going there. He or she forgets, or simply chooses not to consider, that every student's financial needs are different and need affects the cost of attendance.

Some students choose a college because of the football team, proximity to home, reputational excellence for their major of choice, or because they were "sold" on it during the campus tour. Others think schools with the highest price tag are the best, which is not necessarily true. Also, sending their child to a "fancy" school may become a big problem for parents if the school does not provide sufficient financial aid.

Any of these choices may end up being a costly mistake for students and their parents, so they should do their homework before deciding. This also means that it's important to start the school search early enough to get all the financial questions answered. Lack of time and looming deadlines can force families to settle rather than pick.

It is also important to apply to more than one college or university. If a student only applies to one school and doesn't get in, it might be too late to apply to another preferred school for the upcoming school year.

Lack of College Readiness

Lack of academic readiness for college is a concern for higher education officials, but also for high school administrators, government officials, and education not-for-profits. Despite efforts by organizations like the Bill & Melinda Gates Foundation, the National Governors Association, and the College Board, the problem persists.

Many high school students are simply not fully prepared for college-level courses.

The results of the 2012 ACT college-readiness exam showed that only one in four high school seniors meets the four benchmarks designed to prove readiness for a successful freshman year of college, and only 43% of test-takers in 2013 met the SAT's definition of being prepared for college.

What this means is that students are not proficient in college-prep curricula; they are unprepared in reading, writing, and college mathematics, and lack critical thinking and problem-solving skills. These are indicators that they won't be able to keep up with college classes, and therefore are less likely to succeed.

In addition to being academically unprepared, too many students lack clear goals for why they are going to college and what they hope to achieve there.

So what does it mean to be ready for college? In other words, when are applicants ready to get the value of that expensive college education?

Do they have a good mastery of their secondary school education as reflected in SAT or ACT scores?

Do they have good study habits and routines? College is not easy and requires the ability to self-motivate to do quality work on time. If a student can get motivated to graduate early, they can even save themselves or their parents quite a bit of money.

Are they ready to move onto campus? Have they chosen a living situation—dorm, apartment—for convenience and cost?

Do they have a game plan for succeeding in this new environment? There are so many distractions, including homesickness for family and friends, and all the temptations of newly found freedom and independence. College students should have fun, but should prioritize their schoolwork and class attendance. Dropouts and extended college time equals money down the drain.

The Dropout Problem

The college graduation rate in the United States is lower than in many other developed countries. Fewer than 50% of college students graduate within the expected four years.

Students who drop out cost colleges in unpaid tuition, and also cost government agencies that fund financial aid through lower loan repayment rates.

Of course, dropping out means that students don't receive the service for the money that they already paid—no graduation, no degree. Previously paid tuition money is not refundable, but the loans are still owed.

Why are college students dropping out? Besides the lack of preparedness, students drop out due to high tuition fees, lack of commitment, lack of resources, lack of support from family and/ or employer, conflict between school and work schedules, or the stress of balancing work, school, and family responsibilities.

Dropping out costs billions to students in lost future wages, to colleges in lost revenue, and to governments in defaulted student loans.

Not Graduating on Time

Another contributing factor to the cost of a college education is students not graduating on time. College is supposed to be finished in two to four years, but increasingly it's taking longer to graduate. According to the National Clearinghouse Research Center, 54% of undergraduates nationwide are completing, not in four years, but in six. There are many reasons for this, including changing majors too many times, making the wrong choice of school, changing schools but not having transferrable credits, skipping or failing classes, lack of support, taking a leave of absence, and doing internships that take time away from schoolwork.

By taking longer to graduate, students and their parents pay more for that college education.

Complicated Financial Aid Offers

Students enrolling in college need to complete a FAFSA (Free Application for Federal Student Aid) to determine their eligibility for financial assistance. After the application is submitted, the student receives an award letter from the school detailing available financial resources.

This so-called financial aid letter is not truly an aid, but a headache for so many students and their parents. Both the letter and the resources are confusing, with too many options and not enough clear instruction. It's no wonder that students have to rely on the help of professionals to translate their award letter.

Some students think that financial aid is free money. It's not. Financial aid consists of grants and scholarships, which are free and do not need to be paid back, and also loans, which do need to be paid back.

Financial aid letters can confuse students; the amount disclosed as the expected financial aid is always lower than the loans that need to be taken out by the students or their parents. Students don't always realize that they have to take out these loans until it's too late.

Why are financial aid letters so difficult to understand? Fees and expenses are not clearly and exactly disclosed. All costs are not spelled out, and awards look like they are higher than they are. Confusion between grants and loans, the use of abbreviations and fine print, and the option to apply for Plus Loans is unclear. Additionally, different schools format their financial aid letters differently, so it's hard to compare packages from one school to another.

A campaign to standardize financial award letters didn't get the full support from all the schools. They prefer having the flexibility in designing their own letters in their own interest. As only Congress has the power to make this standardization mandatory, in 2012, the National Association of Student Financial Aid Administrators went to Capitol Hill to lobby against standardizing letters.

The financial aid, which is supposed to help students fund their education, instead contributes to its high costs when students are misled during the process.

3

College Debt Is Taking a
Toll on the Economy

As tuition at many colleges and universities continues to increase, so does the number of students and parents taking on more loans; and the size of these loans is rising with the tuitions, with some as large as mortgages.

Students Loans: The Largest
Source of Unsecured Debt

Since 2009, student loan debt has increased at a very rapid pace while other consumer debt has slowed down.

In 2012, according to the Federal Reserve Bank of New York and the National Economic Associates, student loans sat at $914 billion, while auto loans and credit card debt were at $750 billion and $672 billion, respectively. For the first time in US history, student loans topped all consumer loans and became the largest source of unsecured debts.

The Consumer Financial Protection Bureau, created by the Dodd-Frank Act in the wake of the financial crisis, estimated the debt at near $1 trillion at the end of 2011, and passing the $1 trillion mark in 2013. This is $1 trillion in federal student loans and does not include other lines of credit or borrowing from retirement accounts.

According to a recent publication by the Associated Press, more than half of college graduates are either unemployed or underemployed, working at jobs that do not require a college education. They either have no income or insufficient income to repay their debts.

This high unemployment rate combined with the size of their loan debt can lead to a high risk that graduates will default on their loans. All too often, even those who are lucky enough to have jobs can't make ends meet. It's impossible for them to earn enough to live on, much less to pay back their debt. By the time they finish paying their living expenses, they have little or nothing left for student loan payments, which can often be hundreds of dollars a month.

The number of graduates defaulting on their debts is at the highest rate in history. According to an annual publication by the Department of Education, one in ten borrowers defaulted on their payments within the first two years. When students are unable to make their payments, they defer payment for later, or simply ignore the debt. While the delinquency rates vary by the type of institution, the default rate is increasing, surpassing even credit cards delinquencies.

At a greater than 10% delinquency rate, this is having an impact not only on the students and parents, but also on schools and the whole economy as it struggles to come out of the financial crisis.

When students postpone their payments, the time it takes to pay off the loans becomes longer. Students end up paying more in interest on the loans than the principal as the interest accrues over time. In this way a $20,000 loan can easily double to $40,000 or even more.

Even students who have unsubsidized or certain private loans, and those who did not defer their payments, have seen the size of their debt increase significantly over time because of high and accrued interest rates.

Students are at the mercy of debt collectors. Private lenders are known for their aggressive collection tactics. The Department of Education, the largest lender of college loans, often turns to debt collection companies to hunt down the billions of dollars' worth of student loans in default. These companies get paid commissions and other returns on the amount they collect, so they use a variety of tools and techniques, including threatening the defaulters, not giving them options, and violating their rights.

When borrowers default on their loans, their credit scores are affected. They are unable to get other loans or can get them only at higher interest rates. A bad credit score can mean higher insurance premiums, and even not qualifying for certain jobs. Being unable to borrow means deferring some large purchases, which slows down the economy.

In competitive job markets, such as we have now, many employers look at the credit score of the applicants as part of the hiring process. A prospective employee with a bad credit score because of defaulted loans is less likely to get a desirable job. This puts even more pressure on applicants to get rid of their student debts, and to achieve this, they might have to work at jobs that pay but that don't require a college degree. Some students choose majors with tuition assistance, or stay away from majors that tend to accrue a mountain of debt. This can lead to shortages of unskilled professionals or graduates who lack the passion for their chosen livelihoods.

Unemployed or underemployed students or graduates live paycheck to paycheck. They are left with little to no options because of their low credit scores and insufficient incomes. Some turn to payday advance services if they need to borrow to make ends meet. These services charge exorbitant fees and have a high APR, which don't help the borrowers; instead these services bury them further under debt.

Students and graduates with excessive debt are moving back with their parents because they can no longer afford their independence. By staying with their parents, these adult children are saving money, but they may be costing their parents more. Additionally, plans to start their own families might have to wait until their student loan debt is under control.

The Impact on the Economy

Excessive student debt affects everyone. The need to repay the debt means putting off spending on goods and services. Recent graduates can't get ahead by saving and investing for their future. Big purchases like buying a car, starting a business, or buying a house are delayed. It was hoped that younger people— specifically college graduates—would aid the recovery from the financial crisis by purchasing their first homes. But because of the debts they carry, they can't.

According to the National Association of Realtors, there is a drag on the housing market, as young graduates aren't buying houses at the rate the recovering economy needs. With student loan debts in some cases already equivalent to a mortgage, students are failing to qualify for home loans because of low credit scores and unfavorable debt-to-income ratio.

Buying a house was part of the American dream, but many young adults are letting that dream fade away. A survey by Rutgers University found that 40% of graduates delay major purchases like homes because of student loans.

Will College Debt Be the Next Financial Crisis?

At $1.2 trillion and climbing, and with hundreds of billions of loan dollars being defaulted, many are speculating that the student loan problem will follow housing as the next financial bubble.

Before the 2008 crisis, many homeowners owed more on their homes than the actual value of the property. Unable to sell these "underwater" properties, large numbers lost their houses when they could no longer afford to make their mortgage payments.

The situation with student loans is similar. Students and graduates have too much debt and are defaulting on their loans. But unlike a home, which can be repossessed when the owner stops paying the mortgage, a college degree can't be taken away.

The degree to which these loans are a burden to the taxpayer, whether it is a "bubble" or not, is open to debate. But that debate raises other questions about the cost of college, including how much is too much, and what is the value of higher education?

4

The War against Higher Education

D ebt makes life harder and more stressful. A college education—no matter how expensive—used to be considered "good debt," worthwhile for the opportunities that would follow. But now that isn't necessarily the case. For too many people, higher education is creating debt and other issues rather than creating earning potential.

Good Debt or Bad Debt?

More and more students are graduating from college with massive amounts of debt. For too many, the cost of the college education is greater than its value.

That was the case for Anne. After graduation, she owed $1,100 a month toward her college debt. Even working two jobs, she could barely pay her living expenses and was forced to move back home with her parents. Many students find themselves in this situation. For some, it will take 10, 20, or even 25 years to pay off those loans—the same time it takes to pay off a mortgage on a house.

In these cases, college is no longer the gateway to a better life if paying for it leaves graduates struggling to make ends meet.

Then there are students who make the choice not to accumulate more debt and end up dropping out to avoid adding more to what they already owe. They still have debt that needs to be repaid, but now they have no degree and decreased earning power.

In the wake of the recent financial crisis, jobs became scarce, and recent graduates, with their lack of experience, found that even the existing jobs were out of their reach. Expensive degrees couldn't guarantee employment, and many graduates had to settle for any job that supplied a paycheck.

Andrew found himself in that situation. He graduated with a degree in journalism. He looked for a job for over a year, and eventually started bartending at a local bar in the Boston area, making an average $1,300 a week in wages and tips. He simply couldn't find a job in his field that paid as much as what he made as a bartender.

Many recent college graduates work as unskilled labor, such as custodians, cab drivers, parking lot attendants, and assembly-line operators. The Center of College Affordability published a 2013 report that stated 48% of employed US college graduates are in jobs that the Bureau of Labor Statistics suggests requires less than a four-year college education.

Students Loan Debts Affect Graduates and Parents

How would you feel if debt collectors called you, threatening you with prison, every day? That's what happened to Cassandra, who fell behind in her student loan payments because she could not find a job in her field and had to take work at a retail store. She was told that if she didn't pay, she would be sent to jail.

This is just one of the many tactics used by collection agencies. Students are stressed with debt and its effect on their reputation and credit scores. They are unsure how long it will take to pay off the debt, or even if they will be able to ever pay it off in full. To make matters worse, they are harassed by collection agencies and hampered in their ability to have the comfortable life they thought they would have after college. Many are moving back with their parents, settling for jobs just to pay the bills, delaying starting a family, and putting off major milestone purchases.

And it's not just the students and graduates, as student loan debt also affects and stresses the parents.

Parents who cosign on student loans, or who take out Parent Plus Loans, can find themselves trapped by debt. In 2012, federally backed educational loans to parents were estimated at $100 billion, almost 10% of the total outstanding student loan debt. It's an alarming figure, especially to those who borrowed too much, paid with a credit card, cashed out their retirements, or took a second mortgage. And some of those parents are still paying off their own student loans.

According to data published by the Federal Reserve Bank of New York in 2012, Americans aged 60 and over are responsible for $36 billion in student loan debts. They are paying college debt instead of building savings and contributing toward their own retirements.

Student Loan Debt and Its Effects on the Economy

After graduating from college, Luc and his college buddy, Andrew, decided not to hunt for jobs but to make their dream of starting an organic grocery store for their community into a reality. Even though there is a demand for this type of business, the two entrepreneurs were denied business loans everywhere they went simply because they carrying too much student loan debt.

Many other aspiring entrepreneurs find their dreams of starting businesses evaporating because of student loan debt. Small businesses and entrepreneurs are essential to job creation, but student loan debt is preventing them from getting the loans to start the businesses that create jobs and boost the economy.

Leonard thought it was a joke when he received a letter informing him that his paycheck would be garnished and his federal income tax refund taken away. After graduating with a nursing degree, Leonard had moved a few times in search of a better job; his loan statements weren't getting to him, so he was behind on his payments. After several failed attempts to contact the lender, he gave up. His loan was sold, and the new owner found him. Leonard's original loan for $27,800 had ballooned to $43,000 with accrued interest and fees. It will now take Leonard five years to pay off the loan, during which time he'll have to work overtime just to keep from falling further behind.

This is all legal. Lenders, by law, can go after those who are defaulting by garnishing their income and taking away their federal tax refunds. The federal government is also withholding money from a growing number of Social Security recipients. These are retirees over the age of 60 who may be paying for their grandchildren's, children's, or their own loans. A great number of them are defaulting, and, consequently, the government is tapping into their checks.

Nobody would think that Social Security benefits would be subject to withdrawal by a lender, especially the federal government. But lenders nowadays will do anything in their power to collect on student loan debts, and if Social Security benefits are the only thing left, they will go after them.

People with excessive unsecured consumer debt can get a second chance by filing for bankruptcy—but that's not the case with student loan debt. Student loans can't be discharged under bankruptcy unless proven under undue hardship. An increasing number of students and parents are looking at bankruptcy to get a break, but only a very few qualify. But if they can't file a bankruptcy on student loans, they can file on other loans, meaning credit cards and other debt isn't being repaid.

Student Loans Meet Politics

The student loan crisis has become such an issue it has reached Capitol Hill, making it an important tool for many politicians. From campaign promises to debates on the Hill and elsewhere, politicians make promises but fail to come up with solutions. There is simply too much bureaucracy and division among the interested parties.

Why doesn't the federal government enact student loan reform and give a break to those who are struggling? In July 2013, Congress reached a deal to reverse a proposed July 1 increase in the student loan interest rate that would have raised rates from 3.4% to 6.8%. The new plan will tie interest rates to the market, but allow those rates to change over the lifetime of the loan. But despite these efforts, there is still confusion, and nothing has been put forward that offers a long-term solution to the student loan problem.

Movement against High Education

The rising cost of higher education and the crippling debt attached to it naturally creates anger. Higher education is increasingly viewed as a debt trap. Students are told to get some loans, go to school, and life will be better, but for too many that is not what occurs.

Instead, young people don't graduate, or graduate with a lot of debt, can't find the right job, and get harassed by debt collectors while the federal government and lenders make money.

In some instances, while academic cuts are being made at schools, administrators still enjoy their perks, and students have to come up with rising tuition. All these events have triggered student protest—some violent, with students blocking roads or getting into confrontations with the police.

Voices against the higher education system aren't a new development. Taylor Gatto, in his essay "Against School, How Public Education Cripples Our Kids, and Why," published in *Harper's* magazine in September 2003, argued that school is a waste of time. Today, other movements have stirred up anger about the education system and the debt issue.

The Occupy Wall Street movement was born in New York City in September 2011. Occupy's aim was to fight against social and economic inequality by protesting bankers and CEOs who make massive amounts of money while the remainder of Americans barely make anything. Large numbers of recent graduates, many unemployed, joined the movement.

An offshoot of Occupy Wall Street was Occupy College, with students protesting the rising cost of higher education. Students were frustrated because banks got bailed out despite their mistakes that led to the financial crisis, yet students didn't get a break; that frustration could be heard in their rallying cry, "Wall Street got bailed out, but students got sold out." Some of the protesters even hung signs around their necks displaying their amount of debt.

There are many other activists and organizations—both for and against higher education—trying to find solutions to the elevated cost of attending college and university.

Peter Thiel is the billionaire PayPal cofounder and an early investor in Facebook. Thiel made news in 2010 with the Thiel Fellowship, a program that encourages high school students to eschew college or leave school and pursue their own ideas. Thiel provides Fellows with a $100,000 grant and high-profile mentors. The program drew hundreds of applicants and generated a lot of buzz, and more than a few critics. The program's goal is to help students embrace their passions, tackle bigger problems, and most importantly, avoid college debt.

Dale Stephens, a fellow from the Thiel Fellowship, started the Uncollege Movement. Through his movement, Stephens aims to help other students find a path outside the traditional higher education model, by providing them with internships, forums, and trips abroad, and generally challenging them to really learn and build a portfolio of academic and professional work. Stephens established his movement because he felt that students were paying too much for college, but learning very little.

Then there's the flip side to all the graduates who end up working at jobs that don't require a college degree. That would be some of the most successful entrepreneurs and personalities of our time, who didn't go to college or who started and dropped out. These include CEO and Facebook founder Mark Zuckerberg; the late Steve Jobs, the father of Apple; Oprah Winfrey; and David Karp, founder and CEO of Tumblr. These are just a few examples, and they show that college is not the only path to success.

College isn't the best way for everyone. Sometimes hands-on experiences are sufficient or better. Many people follow their passions outside the traditional college landscape and succeed. Some of them do return to school to get the degree as a privilege. Many students graduate and have no clue what they want to do next.

Is college a waste of time? Is it even worth attending? Former United States Secretary of Education, Dr. William Bennett, tried to answer that question in his latest book, *Is College Worth It?* by exposing the broken promises of higher education.

If you still believe higher education is important despite its drawbacks, instead of asking if college *is* worth it, let's instead ask *why* you want go to college and *how* you can get value out of it.

PART II | The Case for Higher Education

5

Higher Education Efforts to Reduce Costs

C riticism toward colleges and universities over the cost of education is mounting. Higher institutions are not deaf to them and are thinking outside the box for ways to control their costs.

From Texas to California and in many other states, tuition freezes have become part of the solution to give students and their parents a financial break. After taking over as president of Indiana's Purdue University in January 2013, Mitch Daniel, former governor of Indiana, froze its tuition. President Daniel argued that instead of asking students to adjust their budget to the university's desired spending, Purdue should try to adjust their spending to the budget of the students and their parents. He plans on continuing the tuition freeze through the 2015–2016 academic years. In-state students will pay $10,000; out-of-state students will pay $28,794. And to further cut costs, Purdue University added higher-deductible healthcare plans and combined or eliminated some administrative positions.

In 2011, Holy Cross College in Notre Dame, Indiana, guaranteed a five-year tuition freeze for students who continuously enroll in a four-year degree program. Other schools, such as Rice University, won't raise tuition at the rate of inflation for continuing students.

Concordia University in St. Paul, Minnesota, Ashland University in Ohio, and Ave Maria University in Florida have actually lowered their tuition fees. Converse College, a small women's college in Spartanburg, South Carolina, slashed its tuition for 2014–2015 from $29,000 to $16,500, a 43% reduction. On its website, Converse College explained the reduction as a way of taking the lead on being a voice of reason on behalf of the students and their families, and as a challenge on the escalating costs of education.

Reducing and freezing tuitions are great first steps to reducing the cost of education. Colleges and universities should also explore ways of cutting prices for room and board.

Flexibility in the Four-Year Degree

Not all students graduate in four years, thus costing them more money for the extra quarter(s), semester(s), or year(s). To reduce costs, some institutions won't charge extra if certain students exceed the four-year timeline required to complete the degree. This program doesn't apply to students who voluntarily exceed the four years by missing classes, failing, or dropping out of school and going back. It's also not for students who aren't sure about their career path or are exploring different majors. It's designed for focused students with clear academic goals, to help keep those students from paying extra for a situation under the control of the school. If a student has to take a course that wasn't available before, putting him or her beyond the four-year limit, the program guarantees that the school will foot the bill.

Midland University, a private four-year college in Fremont, Nebraska, is among institutions offering their own four-year graduation program aimed at boosting the graduation rate and saving students money. Students are required to follow a specific path, declare a major by the beginning of their sophomore year, take their assigned courses, and maintain good grades. In return, the school promises strong academic counseling, to get students into their required classes, and help for them to stay on target.

Many schools are also offering the opportunity to complete a degree in as little as three years, while still enjoying the same benefits as four-year programs. To make this possible, schools have designed curriculum in some majors to fit a three-year time schedule. This means aggressive fall and spring class schedules as well as summer sessions. It's an opportunity for highly focused and goal-oriented students, similar to some intensive accelerated programs that also trim college costs while earning a degree.

In independent study programs, students work on their own, take a proctored examination, and earn credits toward a degree. Some colleges also allow students to test out of classes—but still earn the credits—if they have already studied the materials. This can save hundreds of dollars in tuition, fees, and books.

Some institutions, such as Emory University, Brandeis University, Claremont College, and Stanford University, offer a four-year bachelor's/master's degree program. Students earn credit toward their master's degree while completing their bachelor's degree by taking extra classes during the semester. These schools charge tuition by semester, not course, so the student ends up getting two degrees for the price of one.

Some high schools have even partnered with colleges to develop programs that allow high school students to earn college credits. The Bridge Program, Credit Bank Program, and Early College Advantage Program were all developed with this goal in mind. Although requirements differ from program to program, students basically have to be in junior or senior year, have good grades, and get a recommendation from their high school counselor. Participating students take classes at their high schools or at the participating college, usually free of charge. These programs exist to help students prepare for college, reduce tuition, and manage debt. Imagine starting college with almost one year of college credits earned already, for free!

Look for Debt-Free Colleges

Some colleges give students the ability to attend school without paying tuition; they graduate completely free of college debt.

Davidson College in Davidson, North Carolina, is one of the schools trying to solve the college debt problem by eliminating student loans from their financial aid package. They were able to implement this no-loan policy because of their trust, which covers 100% of the needs of qualifying students.

The College of the Ozarks, a Christian college, also allows students to graduate with no debt. Instead of paying tuition, students work to subsidize their education. The college website's home page states that it's a place where students value God and country and develop character, don't pay tuition, work for an education, and graduate without debt. The school has a low acceptance rate and small enrollment, but the free tuition is a strong inducement for applicants.

Students Are Borrowing Less

As students and their parents are becoming more aware of the issue of college debt, and some institutions are making a concerted effort to reduce tuitions, students are borrowing less.

According to the College Board, the total amount students borrowed fell by 13% for the past few years (2011–2013). Other reasons such as the improvement of the economy, more financial assistance, and lower enrollment have led to students' borrowing less for their college education.

6

Finding Value in Higher Education

Higher education has evolved over the last few decades: tuition is spiking at all an all-time high, students are graduating with crippling debt, "dream jobs" are harder than ever to find, and many graduates are working beneath their qualifications. Despite all this, higher education is still important and valuable for those who prepare for it.

Higher Education Is an Investment

Going to college is an investment, and like all investments, only some will yield good return. They involve risks, have fees attached, and can lose value.

Investors choose to invest in equities, debts, and real estate. Let's say an investor chooses to invest in a particular stock or a mutual fund. He will have to use a brokerage firm or financial professional who will charge a fee on top of the initial investment. If the costs associated with the investment are greater than the return, and if that particular stock depreciates over time, then it's a bad investment.

The same rule applies with higher education. The degree the student chooses to pursue is the product; the institution and its cost of attendance are the fees.

If the cost of attendance is elevated and the student graduates with a degree that isn't in demand and he or she can't be employable, then such education is a bad investment.

Laurie graduated with a bachelor's degree in social science with $34,000 in debt. She was able to get a job that paid her $11.75/hour and struggled to pay her student loans and other living expenses. Instead of getting a second job, she went back to school and got a bachelor of science in nursing, adding $27,000 to her debt. But she was hired to a good job right away, and her employer benefit package included repayment of her student loan.

To get the best return on their higher education, students need to learn to think like a successful investor or businessperson. They must choose the right major that will prepare them for a job that will be in demand three to four years after graduation. And they must examine their colleges of choice very carefully and thoroughly, from the school's ranking to the total cost of attending, including inflation.

The best option is to enroll at an institution that provides not only the most for the money, but also has resources to help graduating students in the pursuit of a lucrative and fulfilling career. A student might choose a degree that he or she has a passion for, whether or not it's in demand, but he or she should still make sure that the cost of earning the degree would not be a burden down the road. The students who get an affordable tuition, earn a scholarship or grant that covers the majority or all of their expenses, and graduate in a field that is in demand are the ones who get the most value out of their higher education.

Higher Education Boosts Earnings

Going to college is still a great move; college graduates earn more than nongraduates. A high school graduate is estimated to earn $1.4 million during his lifetime, while the recipient of a master's degree will earn $2.8 million. By 2020, 65% of all jobs will require postsecondary education.

Cathy was a clerk at a busy auto body shop along with five other associates. She made $12.75 an hour. When Cathy, who had an associate degree in business administration, found out that one of the managers would be retiring in a few years' time, she enrolled in an online class and earned her bachelor's degree in management. When the manager retired, Cathy was promoted and became a salaried employee making $41,000/year.

The US economy is transforming from a manufacturing economy to an economy based on knowledge and skills. Years ago, high school graduates went to work in factories and manufacturing plants. Many of these jobs were outsourced to countries like China as a result of the latest financial crisis. As a result there is now less demand for blue-collar workers and more demand for skilled workers.

Colleges and universities are not just places that develop human capital, but they also play important roles in society, healthcare, and the local and global economy. According to a 2010 report by the World Bank, higher education is a public interest. Worldwide, there is an increasing demand for professionals in the fields of technology, engineering, and medicine. These skills can't be acquired without higher education. Through projects and research papers, higher education also teaches critical thinking, a skill that is crucial to their success both professionally and personally.

Whether they are research universities, professional schools, or liberal arts colleges, institutions of higher education provide many benefits to society. They are places for research, helping solve the world's health issues and other concerns; innovative hubs for ideas; and providers of jobs, directly and indirectly. They assist in developing the community, draw firms and organizations to the area, advise the government on policy and decision-making, and provide cultural and sporting opportunities.

Higher education institutions are vital to the community and beyond. Princeton University alone generates $2 billion in economic activity. And imagine the city of Palo Alto without Stanford University. Palo Alto was established when Stanford University was founded and is now the home of dozens of successful companies, including the largest stem-cell research lab in the world.

Colleges and universities provide invaluable networking opportunities. Students make lifelong friends in college. Peers and professors stay in contact through the years. Schoolmate entrepreneurs founded many businesses.

Overall, higher education is a great asset, improving individuals and developing communities.

PART III | Preparing for College

7

Is College for You?

Why are you going to college?

In case you skipped to this chapter, let me recap: You've been told that after high school, you get a student loan, go to college for four years, graduate, get a job, and reap success. That might have been the case years ago, but things are vastly different now.

Though I still believe higher education is important, I also believe that a four-year bachelor's degree, or higher, is not for everyone.

Some people might only need a two-year associate's degree, an apprenticeship, or even just six weeks of training in a particular in-demand industry. Society needs physicians and engineers, and it also needs truck drivers and welders.

If you feel that college is for you, then you should know why. As I mentioned in the previous chapters, people go to college to

- Become knowledgeable

- Gain skills

- Increase earning potential

- Become informed and productive

- Learn how to think critically

Make Your College Plan

Define your goals. This is how you pursue and measure success. Set some goals, including when, where, and how you want to attend college, and how long it will take you to graduate.

Once you have a clear goal about your higher education journey, develop strategies to reach every milestone. This is where you see just how much passion you have for this pursuit. It's about focusing on your goals to achieve positive results. Strategies can include

- Develop a portfolio

- Take tests to earn academic credits as applicable

- Stay focused on your target GPA

- Get to class on time, work on projects as assigned

- Develop a good relationship with professors and faculty

- Utilize available resources and get connected

- Foster relationships with your professors and faculty

- Join the right groups and get involved

- Know how to study and establish priorities

- Have a set schedule to avoid distractions

- Take summer classes to get ahead

- Decide whether to live on campus or not

How to Choose Your College and Degree

The most important factors in student success in higher education are dedication, the cost of tuition, the major, and the choice of college.

Pick the college that fits your needs and have goals in place that support what you want to achieve in college. This helps you make the best decision. You should make your choice based on

- Academic programs because some schools are well known for certain majors

- The type of school you want to go to: community college, four-year private or state university, or an online degree program

- The academic atmosphere, valuation of degree, and the school's academic ranking

- Graduation rates

- Credit transfers to and from other institutions

- The size of school

- Location: large city, smaller or "college" town, or rural setting

- The resources the institution has available for students and faculty

- The social atmosphere, activities, athletics, and other services offered by the school

- The amount of money the school will cost and also award to you

Don't choose a college just because your friend is going there. Your needs and goals may be different. Talk to alumni and current students or simply browse through online forums. Visit the campus. It's important not to limit your choice to one college; have a backup plan in case your first choice falls through.

One of the main reasons we go to college is to increase earning potential. But in today's economy, industries are changing rapidly, and the degree you earn might become out of date. The course of study you have passion for might not be desirable for businesses when it comes time to apply for jobs. How valuable will your degree be in three, four, six years after you graduate? Will you be employable and have good earning potential with that degree?

There are resources and tools to help you gauge if your college degree path is likely to get you a great income.

PayScale gives you an idea of your future worth and the return on your investment by helping you measure the value of your college education and compare definitions and salaries for hundreds of jobs. The Salary Data, CollegeMeasure, and NerdWallet also offer information on salaries and degrees. NerdWallet breaks down salaries by undergraduate programs.

When choosing your degree, it's helpful to talk to alumni who have completed the same degree, so they can give you feedback. You can also intern or volunteer at jobs related to that degree.

Consult an academic advisor; they are great resources for students. Find out what courses are required to get your desired degree and determine if it is a realistic course load. If you're unsure of your degree, take courses that are common for more than one degree, just in case you decide to switch majors.

What Are Employers Looking For?

A degree is not the only requirement employers are seeking when hiring new grads, especially in a competitive job market. Every employer has a specific skill set for job seekers. In today's job market, applicants with academic disciplines in science, technology, engineering, and manufacturing are especially in demand. But there are other valuable skills desired by most companies, including creativity and the ability to think critically and communicate effectively; literacy, especially in the area of information technology; flexibility, productivity, and the ability to collaborate and work with peers; and leadership skills. These so-called "soft skills" matter more than ever.

The Association of American Colleges and Universities surveyed employers in April 2013 and found that 93% of the respondents value critical thinking, problem-solving, and efficient communication skills more than an undergraduate degree. Some companies even deviate from traditional hiring methods, which are the submission of a resumé and interviews. They go through different routes, like sponsored competitions in which job seekers are asked to solve a problem that's either actually faced by the company or fictionalized just for the purpose of the competition.

BP (British Petroleum) challenged students from around the world to offer innovative solutions to technical problems. The winning contestants were offered paid internships and jobs. An article published by *Business Insider* in April 2013, titled "Google Cares Less about SAT Scores and GPA Because They Have Better Hiring Data," noted how the search engine giant believes that SAT and college GPA don't necessarily lead to any success and "are no longer used as important hiring criteria," said Prasad Setty, Google's Vice President of people analytics.

In addition to the college degree and soft skills, companies look for job seekers who are ambitious, experienced, and have the initiative to go the extra mile to make an impact and difference in their communities.

To recap

- Experience is best, so get an internship.

- Companies like global minds, so make sure to mention if you have traveled overseas through studies, exchange programs, or voluntary work.

- As we live in a global economy, it is an asset to be fluent in at least one other language in addition to English.

- Research the company and know their history, policies, and all information about them. This shows you have interest in the company and are ready to join.

- Social media is a great tool to connect with other professionals and find jobs, especially through LinkedIn. But that same social media can destroy you. Make sure you have updated profiles, positive messages, and professional pictures.

- Google yourself to see what the Internet is saying about you. If you don't, someone else will.

- As you get closer to graduation, spend time in the career center. Get help with resumés, interviews, an internship, and job leads.

- Remember that it's not just about what you know, but whom you know. Beef up your networking skills and get to know people in your industry.

Before we finish our conversation on what businesses are looking for in employees, keep in mind that big corporations aren't hiring enough, but startups and small businesses are the creators of jobs.

8

Be in the Know

With the high cost of higher education, parents and students need to do the necessary research to find out the total cost of attending the school of their choice and determine how they will pay for it.

Financial Aid

One common way for people to pay for their higher education is through the financial aid process. After filing their FAFSA, students receive an award letter that details their personal financial aid package as merit-based, need-based, or non-need based.

The financial aid package, which has grants, scholarships, work-study, and loans, may not always be enough to cover the entire cost at a particular school. This is the reason students and their parents end up needing more loans to satisfy the Expected Family Contribution (EFC), the amount they need to pay out of pocket.

To maximize their financial aid, students must begin the process with the school of their choice as quickly as possible instead of waiting until the last minute. Paul, an excellent student, could have gotten more merit-based money if he had started the admission process earlier, but he delayed, and most of the money was already given away to the students who came first.

While the student finds out the criteria for how schools distribute funds, parents should do their homework by assessing how much they will be paying and if their child will qualify for financial aid based on needs. The Department of Education has a calculator on its website FAFSA4caster.ed.gov that helps parents estimate their family contribution, and a net-price calculator available through the college that estimates financial aid based on each family's situations. Mark Kantrowitz, an expert in financial aid, says that these net-price calculators are invaluable to help families make informed decisions about college affordability.

It's a good idea to choose more than one school when considering paying for college through financial aid. By doing so, the student and parents can compare the total financial aid at different schools, giving them a picture about which school gives more aid.

Some parents or students may not qualify for aid in any particular year, but that shouldn't be a reason to assume that they wouldn't qualify the following year. For many families, income is not guaranteed. Changes affecting the family financial picture might play a positive outcome in getting aid.

The Financial Aid Shopping Sheet

In their effort to educate and inform the consumers through their program Know Before You Owe, the Consumer Financial Protection Bureau and the Department of Education joined forces to create the Financial Aid Shopping Sheet, which schools can use to help students and their parents understand the different types of loans and grants and the amount they might qualify for.

The sheet contains the estimated cost of attendance, which includes grant aid, net price, recommended loan amount, and other valuable information such as the default rate, median debt for completers, and loan repayment information. With all this information, it is possible to negotiate.

Luke wants to go to College A, which offers less money than College B. Luke can now make an informed case to the financial aid officer at College A. If College A wants to keep Luke, it will offer the same deal as College B.

Life situations change, and the financial crisis of 2008 was a good example. Many people lost their jobs and a big chunk (if not all) of their income, retirement accounts, and even their homes. Families get hit with unexpected medical bills, moving expenses, or other events that the financial aid applications didn't take into account. It's important that parents make their case by mentioning unforeseen circumstances that affected their financial life. They can also make an appeal for need-based aid.

Seeking Student Loans

In the event that grants, scholarships, work-study, and institutional aid aren't enough to cover the remaining costs, federal and private loans can cover the remaining balance.

Students should give priorities to federal loans before taking out private loans, which may cost more because of their interest rate. Regardless of whether it's a federal or private loan, research is essential to find out the conditions attached to each loan. Educate yourself on the financial aid terms and know your key financial players.

Ask the following questions to understand your loans:

- What type of loan am I getting?

- Is the interest rate fixed or variable?

- What are the enrollment requirements?

- Do the loans qualify for a repayment option?

- What is the minimum or maximum amount to be borrowed?

- Do payments need to be made while in school?

- Is a cosigner needed in my case?

- Are there other fees that come with the loan?

- What is the grace period?

- How many months or years will it take me to repay the loan?

- Will my projected income be sufficient to make the monthly payments?

Getting a loan is a financial and legal obligation, and that is why the federal government requires entrance and exit counseling. But a financial aid program session helps even more.

Student loans are intended for tuition, books, and room and board. Only borrow what is needed, not more. Experts recommend that the maximum amount students borrow should not be more than their first salary at graduation, and that the loan payments shouldn't exceed 8% of their first-year income.

PART IV | Funding Higher Education

9

Community Colleges Still Win

The rising cost of higher education makes it more and more difficult for many college students to afford traditional four-year programs. It is important for students and families to understand that there are other options. In addition to private or public four-year colleges, there is also the option of the two-year junior or community college.

Without all the bells and whistles of four-year colleges and universities, community colleges prepare students for careers, making them employable and able to earn income. They can also prepare their students to transfer to four-year colleges. But by attending two years at a community college, students and parents save considerably on the more expensive four-year college tuition.

How I Saved Money by Going to a Community College

I started my higher education majoring in accounting at a four-year private university. I have to admit, I wasn't one of the brilliant ones.

One day, after my managerial accounting class, I had a question about the lesson. I was embarrassed to ask the instructor in front of my classmates, as everyone else seemed to understand. So I decided to chase my teacher into the parking lot and ask her to explain it to me. I caught her while she was getting into her car and squeaked out my question. But she told me I should just email her my questions because she was late for her next class— at the local community college.

Curious, I went online and looked at that community college and was surprised to find out how much cheaper it was. So the following semester I transferred there and had the privilege of having the same accounting professor and similar materials, while paying only $50–$70 a credit hour versus $250–$375 at my previous university. And I would be able to transfer my credits after earning my associate degree. I was in heaven. I saved thousands of dollars, and I was still on target for my educational goal.

Going to a community college offers substantial monetary benefits to students and their parents compared to a four-year public or private university. This is quite a boon to those who didn't qualify for financial aid and have to pay out of pocket. According to the College Board, the average published yearly tuition and fees at a two-year public college for in-state students is $3,131, while it's at $8,655 and $29,056, respectively, at a public and private four-year college. With such a relatively affordable tuition, many students are able to pay as they go, avoiding loans and interest.

Additionally, and unlike public universities and colleges, the majority of community colleges don't offer housing for students. Some students perceive that as a drawback. They believe living in the dorms gives them the opportunity to enjoy the college life experience, make new friends, and be closer to classrooms, amenities, and other resources. This is true, but students don't have to live in the dorms to be engaged on campus. Students can live with their parents, or rent a place with other students, usually cheaper than staying on campus. And instead of paying for expensive (and sometimes wasted) meal plans, students can cook for themselves at home and pay only for the food that they actually eat.

So we see that at community colleges, tuition is affordable, with no housing and meal plan expenses. Students are most likely to graduate from community college free of debt, ready to start their career or transfer to a four-year institution where they only have to pay for the remaining time to earn their degree. Add to that the money saved from interest rates that would have been heaped onto their loans.

When April graduated from high school, she wanted to go to the same four-year college as her boyfriend, but her family didn't qualify for financial aid, and her parents would have had to pay a lot for tuition. She opted instead to attend a community college, stayed at home, and completed her affordable associate's degree.

Because of her good academic record and involvement with many organizations on campus, she received a scholarship from a four-year college, where she completed her bachelor's degree at no additional cost.

Other Advantages of Community Colleges

Community colleges afford many advantages in addition to affordable costs and the very real likelihood of graduating debt-free.

Not every high school senior knows what they want to study, and many college students will change their major one or more times. Depending on the school and the changes, this can add classes or even extra semesters to an undergraduate education. For students who don't know what they want to study, a community college can be an opportunity to try different classes and find out what major or course of study is really the right one for them.

Despite criticism that students who attend community colleges don't continue their education, community colleges are great channels for students to complete their higher education by transferring their credits to a four-year institution, and many students do indeed take this route to earning a bachelor's degree. Many community and four-year institutions, private and public, have partnerships allowing for the transfer of credits, especially within state.

If you are planning to go to a community college and then transfer to a four-year institution, check with an academic advisor at both schools to make sure your credits are transferable. Also make sure the four-year institution doesn't require certain credits to be taken in the college, so you don't have to repeat a class.

Four-year college campuses, with their huge size and student population, can be intimidating to some high school graduates. Community colleges are smaller in size, making the transition easier. They have small class sizes compared to four-year institutions, which can have hundreds of students in a class, especially at public universities. With this small class size, it is easier for students to participate, stay engaged, and improve or have good grades, since they don't have to compete academically with so many students.

Applying to a community college removes the stress and scrutiny that comes with the admission process at four-year institutions. Even though there are waiting lists for some classes, students don't have to go through the process of waiting and screening to be accepted at the institution as a whole.

The flexible schedule at community colleges is a plus to many students, especially those with jobs. Students can pick not only the timetable, but also the campus. A good example is the Metropolitan Community College, a community college in the Omaha metro area that allows students to take many classes at any of their four campuses.

Community College Success Stories

After Arthur graduated with his associate's degree in accounting from a local community college, he secured a job working at a private CPA firm. He transferred to a four-year university while working and earned his bachelor's degree in accounting. After graduation, he was offered a better-paying job with a major corporation.

Many students graduate from a four-year institution but can't find a job because they don't have any experience. Arthur's stint at the CPA firm after getting his associate's degree had helped him gain experience, making him attractive to the major corporation.

Community colleges also prepare students to go straight into the workforce, either after a two-year program, or through a shorter program or training. Many community colleges go beyond graduation and offer continuous education to help sharpen skills in different areas. Kevin went to a community college and took two three-hour weekend sessions learning Excel. He then got a job as a clerk.

Society isn't doing a great job promoting the community college and its benefits. Students need to understand and remember that a two-year degree, or short-term training or retraining program, can make them just as employable as a bachelor's degree.

I believe that parents and counselors at high schools need to do a better job in recommending community colleges to students as another alternative to a four-year education. Not every high school graduate is suited to a four-year education. Some of them only need a two-year degree, or specialized training.

Pushing a student to a four-year degree may only result in dropping out, while that same student can get trained in a skilled trade and be a valuable contributor.

Filling the Unemployment Gap

A truck driver with only eight weeks of training and no debt can have an annual income of $42,000—that's value and return on investment right there. But many graduates have a tough time finding jobs because they don't have the skills to be employable.

Companies such as Valmont, Caterpillar, and other manufacturing plants have openings but struggle to fill those positions because job prospects weren't qualified despite their four-year education.

Workers nowadays need skills in the areas of science, technology, engineering, or math to increase their chances of being hired and promoted. A robot technician who has only two years of education also needs to have engineering and computer skills in order to enter precise data and operate equipment.

To help fill this job gap, many city and education officials are taking note and encouraging technical skills training to make graduates employable. The mayor of Chicago announced in 2012 that he planned to reorganize the city's colleges to focus solely on career training for industries likely to provide jobs in the future. In 2013, the $8 million Career Pathways Institute of Grand Island Public Schools in Grand Island, Nebraska, was opened to train students in skilled jobs. Lincoln, Nebraska, is also planning a $25-million facility at Southwest Community College. This is another great example of the way cities are prioritizing the education needed for specialized trades.

With the help of federal funding, community colleges have been increasing skilled trade programs. Companies are also taking the lead in finding solutions to the unemployment issue and solving their biggest challenge: finding skilled employees. They have begun to turn specifically to community colleges to help them train future or current employees with specific skills.

Community colleges are a great way to gain the skills for today's job market, but, most importantly, they are a channel through which to save money and avoid college debt.

10

Investing in a College Education

In our previous chapters, I talked about different ways to pay for college by going to a community college, attending a school that offers free tuition for qualified students, or enrolling in programs that help earn college credits sooner.

While all those are great money savers, college costs are continuing to rise and will continue to do so unless major reforms are enacted for higher education. To keep pace with the costs for future college expenses, many families invest through 529 plans. Parents, grandparents, guardians, or students who have time on their side can benefit by saving for higher education while enjoying the tax benefits.

What Is a 529 Plan?

Investopedia defines a 529 plan as a plan that allows the prepayment of qualified education expenses at eligible educational institutions. I can add that a 529 plan is an investment vehicle that helps students and their families save money to pay for education.

There are two types of 529 plans:

- Prepaid tuition

- College savings

Students and their parents need to make an assessment by identifying how much the college of their choice will cost and how much more they need to save to reach the target before choosing their 529 plan.

Prepaid Plan

Let's say you are a young parent who went to "State University." Your dad attended the same university, as did your grandpa. You want to continue the tradition by sending your son to the same school. You could pay the university at today's tuition rate before your son is even ready for college. The Prepaid Plan allows parents to lock in at the current price and not worry about future tuition increases.

Most eligible universities don't include the cost of room and board as part of the Prepaid Plan. Requirements and limitations also apply depending on the participating schools and states. In general, the beneficiary or the contributor should be a resident, and the amount will vary depending on the age and current grade level of the beneficiary.

Contributions to the Prepaid Plan are made in a lump sum or through installments. Depending on a number of factors, such as the type of contract, the beneficiary's grade, and the current and projected cost of tuition, the program then makes investments that likely meet or exceed the tuition increase for the future date.

Backed by their full faith and credit, most states guarantee that the funds in a prepaid tuition will satisfy the tuition increase, otherwise the state will cover it. The earnings grow tax-deferred and distributions are tax-free and cover the tuition at the beneficiary's school.

But what happens if the beneficiary decides not to attend that particular school? The program can transfer the funds to another institution or to other qualified beneficiaries, but will lose the guaranteed tuition benefits and suffer additional fees. If the plan is canceled outright, the fund loses its earnings and is subject to additional penalties.

The prepaid plan is great for those with 100% certainty of attending a particular school. But due to its restrictions and limitations in covering other college expenses, such as room and board, many students and parents prefer the more flexible College Savings Plan.

529 College Savings Plan

The 529 College Savings Plan offers more choices than the Prepaid Plan. While it doesn't guarantee or lock the future cost of tuition, it's the most-used of the college saving plans because of the investment options and tax benefits. It's a great vehicle to help offset the rising cost of tuition.

Contributions to the 529 College Savings Plan are usually made by parents or grandparents to pay for a beneficiary's future education. A prospective student can also invest in a 529 plan for himself or herself, saving money before heading to college or graduate school. The plan covers all qualified education expenses, including tuition, fees, books and supplies, computer, and room and board.

Through your state, a brokerage firm, or financial professional, you can invest in an education savings plan with different investment options. Some plans allow investment in a portfolio heavy in stocks, if the child is still a baby, for instance. Others may be concentrated in mutual funds, exchange-funds, or a specially designed portfolio whose rate varies based on the average cost of college education. When investing in a College Savings Plan, you could select an aged-based portfolio, with a higher risk and greater return potential if the beneficiary is a child. The asset allocation changes to a more conservative portfolio as the child grows. On the flipside, people can also choose non-age-based investment options, which are more conservative and may yield low returns.

College Savings Plans take advantage of compounding interest. Small amounts contributed to a College Savings Plan can grow over time, especially if invested very early. Let's assume you make an initial investment of $1,000 with a monthly contribution of $125 on a portfolio with a rate of 6.5%. In 18 years, you will have about $54,500. Contributions to this plan can be made through automatic deductions from a checking or savings account.

With a College Savings Plan, the contributor has the flexibility to invest in different investment portfolios based on the risk, the age of the beneficiary, the interest rate, and the current and the projected future cost of education. That is the reason why we have funds with aggressive portfolios and potential high returns, and others have conservative portfolios with a potential low return.

The tax benefits offered through the College Savings Plan are the most rewarding when it comes to saving for college. The earnings grow tax-free and remain tax-free if used for qualified education.

On top of those tax incentives, some states go further by allowing their residents a tax deduction up to the total amount contributed with a limit not exceeding the annual adjusted gross income of the contributor. Other states allow their residents to make a tax deduction regardless of where the resident 529 plan is located.

A College Savings Plan can be transferred tax-free to another plan or to another qualified beneficiary in the event the main beneficiary opts not to go to school. While a Prepaid Plan only applies to a specific school, a College Savings Plan can be used at different qualified colleges and universities, and professional schools and sometimes can cover the cost of schools abroad.

Like the Prepaid Plan, the College Savings Plan has its disadvantages. If the beneficiary is no longer planning to attend college, and if there is no other qualified beneficiary to transfer the plan to, any withdrawal made on a 529 savings plan is subject to a 10% penalty on top of the income tax due on the earnings.

As with any other investment, a College Savings Plan comes with risks. In down markets, the asset can depreciate, losing its value if the portfolio is heavy in stocks. In the same line, a plan with a conservative portfolio won't grow enough to sustain the cost of future education. A 529 plan doesn't guarantee the cost of future tuition and neither is it backed by the state like it is with some prepaid plans.

Beside the investment risk, a 529 College Savings Plan comes with fees and expenses whether it's a state-sponsored plan, through a brokerage firm, or through a financial professional. Fees and expenses such as the enrollment, administration, and maintenance fees vary depending on the type of plan, the plan manager, and the location.

How does investing in a college fund like a 529 plan affect eligibility for financial aid? The FAFSA takes into consideration the College Savings Plan owned by a parent for a dependent student in their calculation. Parental assets are assessed to a maximum rate of 5.6% when calculating the student's EFC (Expected Family Contribution). The 529 plan under the student's name is also assessed at the parental rate of 5.6%, and treated as a parental asset even if it doesn't belong to the parent.

Because the FAFSA doesn't take into consideration the assets of relatives other than parents, many grandparents open 529 College Savings Plans for their grandchildren to avoid the reduction of the financial aid. While this might be a good idea initially, it can also hurt the student later when distributions to the students are treated as income, reducing subsequent financial aid packages. To avoid the problem, the distributions can be held until the student's last year of school.

Despite its flaws, however, the 529 College Savings Plan offers more choices and covers all the qualified college expenses than compared to a Prepaid Plan, which covers only future tuition.

Other Investment Options

Previously known as IRAs and Education Individual Retirement Accounts, a Coverdell Education Saving Account (ESA) is another way to invest for education.

Holders of an ESA can choose different investment vehicles and products, except for life insurance contracts. While contributions to an ESA are not tax-deductible, the earnings grow tax-free and withdrawals aren't taxable if used for qualified education expenses. An ESA doesn't just cover college expenses or higher education expenses, but also covers elementary and high school expenses.

Custodial accounts and Roth IRAs are other ways to save for college with greater advantages than the 529 College Savings Plan or the Coverdell Education Saving Account.

UGMA (Uniform Gift to Minors Act) and UTMA (Uniform Transfers to Minors Act) custodial accounts are channels for minors to own assets/investments overseen by a custodian. Custodial accounts have some tax advantages, but the withdrawn amount can be used for anything, not just education. When the minor reaches the age of maturity, usually 18, the parent or donors can lose control of the trust and the child can decide what he or she wants to do with the money.

The Roth IRA is a popular retirement vehicle for qualified income earners. The Roth IRA takes away the worry of investing in a 529 College Savings Plan if the beneficiary does not go to college. It also gives flexibility of where to invest the money. While a Roth IRA can be used for both education and retirement, it has various tax rules. While the money grows tax free, withdrawals are exempt from penalties if the funds are used for qualified education expenses.

From prepaid tuition, to a 529 College Savings Plan, an ESA, or Roth IRA, students and parents have many options when deciding how to save for college. Each savings vehicle has its pros and cons, so it's very important to analyze each option and see which one fits best with your particular situation.

College Tax Credit

Taxes also play a big role in the choice of a college savings plan. Thanks to Uncle Sam, you can reduce your taxes while paying for college through college tax credits, such as the American Opportunity Credit or the Lifetime Learning Credit.

Formerly known as the Hope Credit, the American Opportunity Tax Credit allows a maximum deduction of $2,500 to an undergraduate pursuing a degree. The tax applies to qualified expenses such as tuition, books, supplies, and equipment. While there are limits on the income and a four-year threshold, this tax credit is a great savings tool.

For both undergraduate and graduate students, the Lifetime Learning Credit allows you to claim up to $2,000 per tax return.

Education Loyalty and Affinity Programs

While they are not college savings plans, affiliate programs also help save money for college by supplementing college savings plans. They allow you to save toward college education by doing what you do anyway on a regular basis: shopping, buying products or services, or through the use of certain debit or credit cards that offer cash rewards toward college funds. Big players like Upromise and Track Purchase give rewards directly to a college savings account of the account holder.

Investing for College or Retirement?

One of the greatest challenges for parents is to figure out how to invest for their own retirement as well as for their children's education funds.

While it's true that it is necessary to invest in a college education, parents should invest the maximum in their retirement account first before the education fund. Retirement doesn't have many options and can't wait, but a student has multiple alternatives such as financial aid, grants, work-study and scholarships.

11

The Beauty of Scholarships

Scholarships play a significant role in helping students pay for their education. Scholarships are financial aid based on the condition of academics, skills, achievements, and other criteria required by the donor(s). Scholarships are free money and don't have to be repaid. People usually think that those with high academic performance, financial need, or great athletic abilities are the only ones who benefit from scholarships. In reality, that isn't the case.

You don't have to have a 225 IQ like Christopher Hirata, who earned a PhD from Princeton at 22 and got a job at NASA; or be a great soccer player like Lionel Messi; or basketball player like LeBron James in order to win a scholarship. There are wide ranges of scholarships available for everyone, even average students, including many that you probably never thought about.

Types of Scholarships

The most common scholarships are based on academics, financial need, athletics, or community service. But there are also scholarships for minorities, sexual orientation, church affiliation, first-generation students, farmers, and those ill with certain diseases, to name just a few.

Scholarships come from institutions, corporations, professional and social associations, church groups, religious groups, nonprofits, private donors, and individuals interested in supporting a specific cause.

The Aaron Gregory Riley Scholarship was established in honor of Aaron Gregory who died from an accidental drowning caused by an epileptic seizure. His father raised money and started a scholarship to aid young people living with epilepsy. The scholarship awards $5,000 annually to an eligible Ohio Wesleyan student with epilepsy.

Many families establish scholarships to honor and remember their loved ones and to support others with the same condition or situation. Many scholarships are related to diseases. If you are a student who has suffered or is suffering any kind of disease, make an effort to research with your school or organizations affiliated with your disease to see if there are any scholarships available to you.

I was amazed when I read the story of Major Dan Rooney and the scholarship money for Fallen Soldiers' Children. Major Rooney, after seeing a family on a tarmac with the flag-draped coffin of a soldier killed in Iraq, decided to make an impact. Major Rooney, a professional golfer, began raising money for survivors with the help of other golfers and corporation partners. His foundation, Folds of Honor, has funded over 5,000 scholarships for families of fallen soldiers.

Scholarship Sources

Scholarships exist in many areas and situations of life that you might not have heard of. But how can you find scholarships?

If you are a high school student heading for college, your starting point should be your high school counselor, who will most likely have information pertaining to scholarships suitable for your needs and your future goals. If you are already a college student, your financial aid/career center or the college libraries are great places for your search.

Depending on your degree, especially if you are in a high-demand field, you should be able to find financial assistance. For instance, if you are pursuing a degree in accounting, the American Institute of Certified Public Accountants offers many scholarships for students of accounting at different times during their academic careers in addition to what their state and local CPA societies might offer.

It's always a good idea to think local first. Visit your local library reference section or check out books that have information about scholarships. Find out if the different local organizations and nonprofits in your town have scholarships that meet your criteria. Don't forget your parents' employer or yours, if you work for one. Many employers or corporations offer scholarships to support employees, their families, and the residents of the cities where they do business. Scholarships can also be found through federal agencies. For example, the Department of Homeland Security offers a variety of prestigious scholarships for those who want to pursue a career in the areas of cyber security, information technology, management, emergency management, policy, and law. Beyond those resources, as we live in the digital age, the Internet offers a wealth of information when it comes to the search for scholarships that are tailored to you and your needs. Websites like Fastweb.com, Collegeboard.com, and Scholarships.com put information about thousands of scholarships at your fingertips.

Having a strategy as you search is helpful. To avoid wasting money and time searching and applying for scholarships you don't need or won't qualify for, Fastweb.com, does the job for you. You simply enter information about yourself, from your intended major, to your skills, which school you want, and the year you need the scholarship. It then matches you with the available scholarships. The website can even automatically email you information when it becomes available.

To find and apply for the right scholarship, you will need to identify what is unique about you and that qualifies you for a scholarship. African-Americans or Hispanics can apply for scholarships that encourage minorities to attend college. The First Generation College Scholarship is for applicants who are the first in their family to apply to college. Some banks offer scholarships—inquire where you have your account. Some cellular phone providers also offer scholarships. Service organizations, like the Rotary Club or the Junior Chamber International, have scholarships, as do several organizations who offer Patriotic Scholarships.

Animal lovers, victims of bullying or antibullying activists have scholarships (the latter through Abercrombie & Fitch). Local TV stations offer scholarships—the cable network C-SPAN runs a national video documentary contest worth $50,000 in scholarship. The Jif Peanut Butter Sandwich Scholarship awards a $25,000 scholarship for the best peanut butter recipe. The Duct Tape "Stuck at Prom" Scholarship awards up to $10,000 for wearing duct tape to prom.

However amusing some of these may sound, scholarships, while free, aren't just handed out like candy. Applicants need to employ effort in searching out and applying for those funds.

Scholarship Successes

Just before her senior year in high school, Ali began looking at how she could pay for her college education. Her parents could not afford her tuition, so she turned to her school counselor for advice on the available scholarships for which she was qualified. She applied for a few scholarships, including The Susan T. Buffett Scholarship, which is funded by billionaire investor Warren Buffet. She researched the foundation and talked to past recipients to get their insight and advice. Because of her grades, extra curricular activities, volunteering in the Omaha communities, letters of recommendation, and her written application, Ali was awarded a full ride scholarship to attend the University of Nebraska–Omaha.

Ali believes that her community service and application essay played a key role in winning the scholarship. Ali wrote about pursuing her education in neuroscience, an area she is passionate about, so she can help solve problems associated with the brain.

Inspired by his own mom, who attended college with no debt thanks to scholarships, Nick applied for scholarships from high school even before his junior year in high school ended. Nick's goal was to get help to pay for his tuition, books, and board. By applying for multiple scholarships, Nick was able to reach his goal. With awards ranging from just $250 up to $10,000, Nick received a total of $31,000 in scholarships. Nick made the commitment to research and apply for at least five scholarships every school quarter. He treated it like a part-time job, and it paid off.

When it comes to scholarships, students need to understand that it requires extra time and effort to find and apply for scholarships. This is in addition to the hard work dedicated to maintaining good grades.

From Ali and Nick's experiences, here are some valuable points:

- Apply early, so you don't rush to meet the deadline. Rushed applications are rarely as well-thought-out or written.

- Scholarships aren't just for high school and college students; students in elementary school can also apply.

- Apply to as many scholarships as you can. You are not the only one applying, so maximize your chance of getting something.

- Make sure you are eligible before applying; otherwise, it's a waste of both your time and the organization's.

- Research the sponsoring organization.

- Write a concise essay but let your passion show through.

- Google yourself and make sure you have a positive online image. To avoid any surprises, Ali didn't have a Facebook profile. She had only a LinkedIn page.

- Be disciplined and dedicated when searching and applying for scholarships.

- Be committed and don't give up because you didn't get a particular scholarship. Look for other ones.

- Follow the money. If you know of big and recent endowments, seek that scholarship.

- Be engaged by serving your community. For example, the Junior Chamber International has chapters in many US cities and around the world, offering volunteer opportunities to young adults.

Scholarship Fraud

As an endnote to this discussion on scholarships, it's important to acknowledge scholarship scams out there that promise guaranteed scholarships and insider fast-tracking or favoring in exchange for payments made by students and parents through cash or credit cards.

Be careful. Scholarship organizations make the final decisions as to which students they award financial assistance. Legitimate scholarships do not require fees or your credit card information either. The purpose of a scholarship is to save money, and if you have to pay fees, then it's not probably a real one.

Scholarships help many people pay for their education so they can avoid college debt, but other alternatives give students a leg up and help pay for college as well.

12

Alternative Ways to Pay for College

Not everyone wins scholarships and financial aid. Borrowing money remains the most common way to pay for college.

Interest on federal student loans is fixed between 4.6% and 7.2%, depending on the types. Private loans are usually more costly because rates are not always fixed and tend to be higher anyway.

But there are other types of loans, with little or no interest, that are offered by some states, charities, colleges, nonprofits, startups, and alumni.

Low- and No-Interest Loans

Mounting interest can drastically increase the amount of an outstanding debt. Interest-free loans take that worry away. Students only owe the principal, the amount borrowed.

The State of Massachusetts offers a no-interest loan to Massachusetts residents pursuing a post-secondary education with a $4,000 annual maximum and $10,000 lifetime limit. The Military Officers Association of America offers loans for up to

$5,500 to the children of officers. The Student Education Loan Fund, based in Livermore, California, and funded by local Rotarians, lends money at 0% to college students and those in training for a service profession. The fund is supported by donations and payments from other students.

Qualifying Students Can Also Apply for Low-Interest Loans

The Common Bond aims to make education more accessible by lending money to students at lower rates than currently offered by the traditional student loans market. Co-founded by David Klein, an alumnus of Wharton Business School, Common Bond lends money to students in loans sourced from alumni, private investors, and institutions. The company funds millions of dollars of student loans while helping investors earn financial return.

Tom Sharbaugh, an attorney and 1973 graduate of Penn State, started a micro loan program for students. His approach is a little different: with the help of the alumni, he loans money to students who have financial woes or need emergency cash.

North Dakota offers loans at the fixed rate of 5% to its residents and 6.4% to students from the five neighboring states who qualify.

Another startup that helps students is Lumni. It does things a little differently. Founded on the belief that there is a better way to assist students in paying for their education, Lumni doesn't offer loans. The company helps you pay for college. In return, and after you graduate and have a job, you start paying back a percentage of your salary for a set period of time.

While no- and low-interest rate loans can help you with college, students and their parents need to do the homework and learn everything they can about the repayment plans. Student federal loans might have a high rate compared to no- and low-rate loans, but they offer more flexible loan repayment plans and relief to students who find themselves in difficult situations.

Show Your Entrepreneurial Spirit

When Mark Zuckerberg and his roommates founded Facebook (then Facemash), he had no idea it would become a billion-dollar company. Zuckerberg dropped out of college in favor of building what he believed would be a lucrative company, much like Bill Gates did (although Gates did eventually go back and earn his degree). Paying for tuition won't be an issue for Zuckerberg in the event he decides to go back to school.

More students than ever are taking the entrepreneurial route to fund their education. With the help of the Internet, social media, the proliferation of apps and support at their own colleges, students are founding their own companies. Some drop out and focus on their business; but many others stay in school, build their businesses, and use the profits to pay for their education.

That is what happened to Matt, whose school project became a real business. In high school, Matt was asked to write a marketing plan for economics class. As part of his project, Matt identified a need for a landscaping service in the subdivision where he lived in Greensboro, North Carolina. His neighbors were older; they needed help mowing. Matt decided to create the business himself and continued to build it through college, growing it from one to 18 employees. He paid for college from the profits of his landscaping business and didn't have to worry about college debts. After college he sold his business at a good profit to pay for graduate school at Temple University.

Many organizations award students for their business ideas, innovation, and creativity. The National Collegiate Inventors and Innovators Alliance provides early stage funding of up to $75,000 so student entrepreneurs can bring their ideas and concepts to life. Students can also compete by pitching their ideas or submitting their business plans, with an opportunity to win money to start their business. Alexa Von Tobel, CEO of LearnVest, a leading financial planning website geared to women, won a business plan competition that helped her launch her company.

Through elevator pitches, business plans, and innovative ideas, students can win grants, prizes, products, and other services sponsored by different organizations, companies, and their schools. Most funds are geared toward launching and building the business, but cash prizes can also be unrestricted for their use, whether students intend them for tuitions or other expenses.

Study Overseas

Why should you cross national borders or go overseas to study when you can do it here? The answer is simple: you can find bargain prices at colleges and universities abroad.

Many public universities in Europe are free for students from the European Union, and affordable for international students. But Norway offers free tuition to all students at their public colleges and universities because higher education is publicly funded. Foreign students in Norway can enjoy the same privilege of free tuition, no matter which countries they come from. Students interested in studying abroad should research public university systems in other countries in Europe, as well as in Africa, South America, or Asia where tuitions are free or affordable. Check if those countries have any educational partnerships with the United States or other governments.

Studying overseas doesn't necessarily mean spending your entire undergraduate career in a foreign country. Many foreign universities have partnerships with US universities where students can study for a year, semester, or during the summer and earn credits for much less money than they would have paid through a US college.

There are also scholarships dedicated to exchange students and those who want to study and experience living in a different country. US students willing to study overseas as part of the Fulbright Institute twinning program, an educational partnership between the US and India, can earn up to $20,000 a year. But they have to major in an area of interest to the US government. Likewise, Stephan Schwarzman, chairman of Blackstone, a private equity firm, founded the $350-million Schwarzman Scholars Program. The program covers an all-expenses-paid one-year master's degree at the prestigious Tsinghua University in Beijing in the area of public policy, business, international relations, or engineering.

Companies want employees with a global mind exposed to different countries. Microsoft alone employs a large number of students from the Indian Institutes of Technology. Studying overseas helps save money for college and also gives you the opportunity to learn a new language, discover new cultures, and be highly desirable to global companies.

The Military Route

We all have a love for our country, but if you wish to do more, you could join the military and get help with your education.

The Army offers a range of benefits including financial assistance toward education. But the Army can also provide financial assistance to those who have student debts. The financial aid comes in different forms: scholarships, grants, and bonuses, depending in which area of the Army the students enroll. The most popular are the Montgomery GI Bill, the Post 9/11 GI Bill, and the ROTC program.

The US Air Force ROTC program provides scholarships to high school and college students, available through many campuses.

It's important for those who are seeking such financial assistance to check with the military recruiter or job counselor and be aware of the conditions that apply.

Work and Pay for Your Own Degree

I finished college debt-free because I worked to pay for most of my college education. After graduation from a community college, I took some time off, worked, and saved money before I headed back to the university to get my bachelor's degree.

Many students take this approach of working and paying for their own education. While it may not be easy with every degree, it is possible, especially for undergrads. Zac Bisonette, author of *Debt-Free-U*, graduated without loans by working and paying for his education. Not only do the students who work and pay for college education save money, they also manage their time better and are more disciplined.

Owen made it a goal to find an employer who would pay for his college education. For him, the benefits offered by a company were more important than the pay. He graduated free of debt because his company paid up to $8,000 a year in tuition reimbursement. Then after graduation his company was reluctant to pay for his graduate school because the course of study didn't fit with the company. So Owen got a job at the local private university and received free tuition as part of his benefits package. He graduated having paid for almost nothing except for his books and some fees.

Many employers still offer education assistance. They give money to employees to go to school. Tuition reimbursement is usually an investment made by the employer who expects a return on the investment through the employee's gained skills.

The perk of tuition reimbursement isn't completely free. Employers may have requirements, such as maintaining a certain GPA and working for the company for a certain period of time. Others are more flexible and don't demand that employees stick with the company. Starbucks, already known for providing healthcare coverage to even its part-time workers, made news when it announced that it would help thousands of baristas pay for their college degree at Arizona State University.

Some companies, like United Technologies, also offer significant tuition benefits to their employees, paying up to $45,000 for undergraduates and $65,000 for graduate students. Offering tuition assistance is a way for companies to attract, develop, and retain talents. Be smart and look at the benefits, not just the paycheck.

PART V | The Revolution of Online Education

13

Savings Through Digital Education

Not all college students go to school full-time. Many students attend part-time while they are working or caring for their children (or other family members), or have dropped out and are now returning to school. It is becoming increasingly common for these non-full-time students to pursue their education through online programs. Online courses are more flexible, increasingly accessible, and often more affordable.

Online Degrees

Online education is no longer only for a nontraditional student. From their homes, offices, vacations—from almost any location where the Internet is accessible—students can complete their degree at any time at their own pace.

As an alternative to the hefty price of college education, especially at traditional schools, many students are turning to online degree institutions. According to a report by the Babson Survey Research Group, enrollment in online college courses continues to rise. Their 2013 Survey of Online Learning reveals that the number of higher education students taking at least one online class has now surpassed 7.1 million.

Traditional colleges and universities have taken note and embraced the online education model so they can satisfy the needs of students. Universities and colleges now compete with each other to offer a growing selection of online classes. Some schools partner with other institutions to deliver these digital courses. Thunderbird School of Management, for example, merged with the online Laureate Education, Inc., to offer online classes. The University of Phoenix, Kaplan University, Devry University, Liberty University, and Bellevue University are some of the leaders in the online education field. They are known for their online degrees, and they have large enrollments of online students.

While University of Phoenix offers online and on-campus courses, Western Governor University, another leader in the industry, only offers the online component. Founded in 1997 by a group of 19 governors to expand access to higher education, the Western Governor University (WGU) offers courses in business, teacher education, and information technology. It has become a popular destination for students who have dropped out of school and want to go back but need a flexible schedule, as well as for those who just want to save money.

At WGU, students pay by the term, which runs six months, not by credits. With a $2,890/term basic tuition for most programs, WGU is less than $6,000/year. *Time* magazine called the WGN "the best relatively cheap university you've never heard of."

Saving Opportunities with Online Degrees

Online degrees offer savings opportunities. Thanks to the Internet, schools can offer online classes, making higher education accessible and affordable to students. New ways of delivering lessons, such as streaming videos or on-demand courses, also play a role in the effectiveness of the growing online education. A student serving on an Army base in Germany can enroll in an online course through Bellevue University in Nebraska, taught by a professor located somewhere on a beach.

An online institution can increase its revenue by attracting and enrolling many students from different geographic areas, while a brick-and-mortar institution is limited to the number of students it can accommodate. Online education offers savings opportunities for both the institution and the students. Online institutions avoid the cost of maintaining a building, overhead costs like insurance and utilities, many administrative expenses, printing costs, expenses related to weather issues, and cafeteria expenses. Going online allows colleges to charge students affordable tuition. Students taking online classes save on on-campus housing, meal plans, concierge services, transportation to campus, relocation expenses, impulse buying on campus, parking fees, and books and supplies.

Most schools—not only online colleges—are shifting to online textbooks and e-books, helping students save money on expensive textbooks. This also reduces schools' budgets on supplies. Reducing or eliminating the cost of books and supplies saves money for both the students and the schools.

Aside from savings, flexibility, and accessibility, online education also allows students to interact with their peers from all over the country, even the world, and to learn from them.

When I was taking my international accounting class online, I figuratively rubbed elbows with students from different backgrounds and life experiences, including older adult students already working in the field.

Students can watch an instructor's live presentation or a recorded video and watch it again as he or she desires. There is no wait for the instructor to grade quizzes and exams; test results can be instant. Online institutions offer great online resources, accelerated programs, and degrees relevant to today's job market as it evolves the need for new skills.

Despite many advantages offered by online degrees, however, students need to carefully choose their institutions and stay disciplined when taking online classes.

How to Choose Your Online School

Choosing an online institution depends on the goals of the student and what he or she intends to do with the degree. Some students take courses they can transfer to another school, while others simply intend to earn degrees online and advance in their career.

With the rather dizzying proliferation of online classes and degrees, students should be careful in choosing where to attend.

- Check to see if the school is accredited by the US Department of Education to ensure other institutions or potential employers recognize your credits.
- Investigate the reputation of the school.

- Online educational institutions charge tuition in different ways. Verify if you will be charged by credit, by semester, and whether they offer financial aid.

- Taking online courses requires basic computer knowledge, but not everyone is tech-savvy. If you will need technical assistance, make sure your school has a helpline or live chat help.

- Verify that your computer and other tools are compatible to take courses, quizzes, and exams.

14

Higher Education on the Cheap

There is a new type of online degree program offering free courses to students around the world.

What wasn't possible just a few years ago is now a reality: college and advanced level courses are now available anywhere with people from around the world. Renowned professors and experts in the field, stemming from top-notch universities, teach most of these classes. Students can even receive certificates and credentials from some of these elite schools.

The beauty is that most of these online courses are free or really, really cheap. They are called MOOCs.

So What Is a MOOC?

Although the MOOC has become popular and has attracted millions of students from around the world during the past three years, it's still relatively unknown. MOOC stands for Massive Open Online Course, and like the name states, the MOOC is an online course with many participants from different geographic areas. The online course is accessed on the web for free through videos, forums, and other tools.

But let's understand the four words of the term MOOC:

- Massive: available to anyone from anywhere and can accommodate thousands of students taking the course at the same time.

- Open: available to anyone without the hassle of the admission process.

- Online: totally an online class, not a hybrid or a blended online program.

- Course: they are courses, not just a video to watch at the student's leisure. Courses have a start date, a curriculum, and an end date.

MOOC is aimed at making education affordable, and accessible and to change the way courses are delivered.

Innovation Meets Higher Education

Airbnb, a community marketplace in which people may rent a room, a house, or even a castle, is disrupting the hotel industry. Aero, aimed to improve the way people watch television, was a threat to the cable industry until the court put a brake on its advancement. In the same way, the MOOC and its pioneers disrupt and change the traditional education system and make it affordable. With high-speed Internet, social media, cloud computing, and other valuable tools, content can be delivered efficiently and cheaply, thus making online courses reliable, easy to access and far less expensive.

The MOOC embraces innovation by offering courses tailored to today's in-demand skills. While some pioneers started the idea of the MOOC a while ago, Sebastian Thrun was the one who shined the light on the massive open online education when he founded Udacity.

Well known in Silicon Valley, Sebastian Thrun taught computer science and electrical engineering at Stanford University. With his wealth of knowledge in robotics and artificial intelligence, he founded and led the Google X Lab. Thrun challenged the world by becoming the man behind Google's driverless cars. After that success, he wanted to disrupt another industry: higher education, which he believes is inefficient, ineffective, and costly. His idea of creating a universal low-cost education and revolutionizing higher education became a reality when he co-founded Udacity, one of the first MOOCs.

With the backing of investors and other professors, Udacity was founded as an independent education online platform that provides inexpensive higher education to virtually anyone. With a clear and simple mission to bring accessible, affordable, and engaging higher education to the world, Udacity teamed with universities such as Stanford University to offer courses that are important to our changing world.

Education is no longer a one-time event, but a lifelong journey. Thrun is considered the godfather of free online education. His boldness and his success with his first class inspired others to embrace the concept of free massive open online courses.

After Udacity was founded in January 2012, many other MOOC institutions followed, including Coursera, Edx, and Udemy. These free online education platforms, while pursuing the same goal of free tuition to the masses, vary in terms of the type of venture, their partnerships, types of courses offered, and the number of students enrolled.

The Ivy League universities raced to partner with MOOC institutions to deliver online courses. Others created their own free online platform. Today, you can take free courses from top-notch universities through the Harvard Free Course, Yale Free Course, and many others. No wonder many higher institutions are becoming more interested in the free online education movement. They see the value in these courses and want to expand their brand to the millions of students worldwide.

Even though higher education is regulated and subsidized, it sees online education enabled by the Internet as a threat. Campus- and classroom-based institutions of higher education are facing the risk of becoming irrelevant or obsolete. Look how the online giant Amazon brought down Borders bookstore. Higher education must exist in the digital world, even if just by offering online classes, in order to avoid being replaced by it.

The providers of MOOCs are developing partnerships not only with brick-and-mortar higher institutions, but also with companies and organizations such as Facebook, Salesforce, AT&T, the federal government, National Geographic, and even the World Bank.

MOOCs Versus Traditional Colleges

As the MOOC institutions have gone so far connecting students, companies, and organizations globally, traditional college leaders are scratching their heads. They are thinking about their own future, wondering if the MOOCs will replace traditional higher education.

Defendants of the traditional college system argue that an online degree isn't a fit for all and that MOOCs aren't the way to stay educated. They believe that in order to be successful, students need to come together and connect through real-life experiences on campus with peers, professors, and faculties. They believe that employers will be more reluctant to take an online course or degree from any of those providers seriously because there isn't serious testing or exams. Then comes the issue of accreditation, which MOOCs lack, thus calling their quality and value into question.

But let's keep in mind that there are higher institutions that are accredited, but still deliver poor results, have a high dropout rate, poor teaching methods, low enrollment, and, of course, high tuition.

Is Accreditation Synonymous with Quality in a Course?

If many students around the world are enrolling in the MOOCs courses, and if brick-and-mortar institutions and organizations are rallying with the MOOCs, they must be seeing value in the system. Students today can have access to education from Ivy League colleges and award-winning professors through MOOCs, which wasn't possible years ago. A study from the Department of Education shows that online learning can be as effective as classroom learning. The MOOCs are challenging the traditional higher education setting by bringing courses and content that prepare people for today's jobs. Even the Khan Academy, a success story of online video tutorials, has proven successful in helping people build vital skills.

MOOCs make higher education courses accessible, at no cost to the student. Once they figure out the issue of accreditation and testing, they could easily take traditional colleges out of business. Until then, they are great ways to increase skills and learn for life.

PART VI | Managing College Debt

15

Loan Repayment Plans

To avoid the painful consequences that come with student debt, many schools, organizations, lenders, and the federal government have put payment plans in place to help students manage their college debt.

Tuition Payment Plan

Many schools offer a tuition plan in which students can make monthly payments while they are still in school. Students enroll in the plan by paying a one-time annual or semester fee, depending on the length or duration of their courses. Tuition payment plans are short-term. An annual tuition can be divided into twelve equal payments or fewer, whatever is convenient and affordable for the student. Enrollment is easy, usually online.

If your college or university doesn't offer a tuition payment plan, do some research at your financial aid office to see which organizations provide such services; but be sure to also understand their rules, how the service works, and the fees.

Tuition payment plans can be highly advantageous to students. They are affordable (payments are small), they decrease or do away with post-graduation debt, there is no interest added to the tuition costs, and they are flexible and convenient (students can set up automatic payments from their checking or saving accounts or from a credit card).

Loans Repayment Plans

Imagine having an outstanding student loan debt of $325,000 and a salary of $52,000. These mortgage-sized debts are the reason so many graduates are missing their payments, dropping loans in delinquency, or defaulting outright.

College debt can't be discharged under bankruptcies.

Loan repayment programs were created to help borrowers struggling to keep up with their student loan payments. Instead of ignoring student loan payments during difficult financial times, students can find temporary relief through deferment and forbearance.

Deferment allows students to postpone their student loan payments for a period of time, usually for a year at a time. Students with subsidized loans don't pay their interest rate, but others with unsubsidized loans will have their interest added to the principal at the end of the period. To qualify for deferment, students must meet certain criteria, like facing a temporary economic hardship, unemployment, being a half-time student, or on active duty in the military.

Forbearance can reduce a student's monthly payments or postpone them for up to five years. Unlike the deferment option, students who qualify under the forbearance have to pay interest rates on their loans whether or not it's subsidized or unsubsidized.

The following plans are for students struggling to pay their federal loans:

- The Standard Plan—Students make equal payments for ten years. Students can save money on interest charges by paying off the loan quicker.

- The Graduate Plan—The Graduate Plan allows students to make lower payments first and higher payments later for over a period of ten years. This plan is especially workable for students who expect to increase their earnings over time.

- The Extended Repayment Plan—To qualify for the extended repayment plan, student borrowers must have an outstanding debt of at least $30,000. Students then make fixed monthly payments, or start small and increase the amount, for a maximum of 25 years.

- The Income-Based Repayment Plan—Monthly payment is limited based on the borrower's income and family size, a big relief for those who have high payments but low incomes or families to support. After making payments for 25 years, the remainder of the loan is forgiven.

- The Income-Contingent Repayment Plan—This plan is similar to the Income-Based Repayment option, but the monthly payment is calculated based on the borrower's adjusted gross income, the family size, and the amount of the direct loan. Payments can be made up to 25 years.

- The Income-Sensitive Repayment Plan—This plan is for borrowers who don't qualify for the Income-Contingent Plan. Under this plan, the borrower chooses a fixed monthly payment between 4% and 25% of their gross income.

- Direct Consolidation Loan—The federal government allows borrowers to consolidate all their federal loans into one loan and extend repayment to as long as 30 years. Under the consolidation program, students pay a lower monthly payment, but end up paying more because consolidation may increase the length of the repayment.

Critics argue that the process of qualifying for a repayment plan is too long, with too much bureaucracy and paperwork. Others make the point that struggling students don't know about the options because the federal government doesn't promote the plans. Another complaint is that the repayment plans are limited to loans taken during a certain period of time, and not available to all the borrowers regardless of when they took their loan.

Despite these criticisms, the federal loan debt management plans still have a great advantage over private loans, which don't offer much in terms of relief to the borrower.

The Dark Side of Private Loans

CNN reported the story of grieving parents hit with a $200,000 student loan debt for their deceased daughter. They had cosigned a $100,000 loan for her, which became $200,000 after her death as a result of fees, penalties, and a 12% interest rate. The story got people concerned about college debt, especially debt from private loans. After the national attention and petitions, the lender gave relief to the family by reducing the interest rate and the amount of one of the loans.

Most private lenders don't offer repayment plans to borrowers with financial hardships. If the family in question had federal loans, their debt could have been discharged, or they could have at least received assistance or qualified for a payment plan. Federal loan programs offer some alternatives, but with a private loan, you aren't guaranteed any assistance.

How to Manage College Debts

Choosing the right payment plan is critical in managing debt. It is one thing to qualify for the plan you want, and another to understand the plan and how repaying the loan will affect you in the long run.

For some an income-based plan, which allows low monthly payments and forgives the rest of the loan after a certain period of time may be best. For others, a consolidation plan that bundles all federal loans into one plan with a lower payment may be more suitable.

Choose carefully; the right plan will really give you the relief you need.

- Track your loan: Know your loan servicer while you are in school and after you graduate. Make sure they have your correct contact information. If you move, provide them with your updated information so that you don't miss statements and get behind on your payments.

- Know the type of loans you have, and the conditions that apply, such as when repayment starts, and if you qualify for any modified plans in case you get into a tough financial situation.

- Ask for help: If you have federal student loans and have financial hardship, see if you qualify for deferment or forbearance, giving you a break from repayments. If your loans are from a private lender, reach out to them and explain your situation. Negotiate with them on the maximum you can afford to pay now. They'd rather have you paying something than not paying at all and defaulting.

- Put your payments on automatic mode: By setting up automatic payments from a checking or savings account, you will get a bonus of a quarter percentage off your interest rate on federal loans.

- Refinance: Although you can consolidate your federal loans, refinancing your loans, especially high-interest-rate private loans, into a lower-interest-rate loan, can be a great money saver. Research deals that offer low interest rates, and make sure to understand the conditions that come with those new loans. Startups like SOFI can help many students refinance their loans. SOFI brands itself as the leader in the student loan-refinancing arena and has provided more than $840 million in loans. Refinancing can help students save a lot of money depending on the new rate.

16

Student Debt Forgiveness Programs

Even better than repayment plans are student loan forgiveness plans. The federal government, some local governments, organizations, and employers offer students loan forgiveness to those who qualify.

Student loan forgiveness "forgives" a portion or the whole amount of a student's loan. As it's becoming more difficult or impossible for students to pay their loans, student loan forgiveness plans are a great way for qualified students to increase purchasing power once their loans are reduced or eliminated.

The federal loan forgiveness program is the most common, allowing students to reduce or wipe out their student debt, depending on the type of loan.

Under the Obama Student Loan Forgiveness Plan, students who have made regular payments on their federal student loans for over 20 years can have the rest of their payments forgiven.

This program is a continuation of the repayment plan and allows students to get a financial break after those long years of payments. It is still difficult for some students to fully pay their debt after the repayment plan, so loan forgiveness is great option that clears the outstanding debts.

Keep in mind that this federal student loan forgiveness plan only applies to federal loans, not private loans.

There are different student loan forgiveness programs under the federal student loan program, all of which discharge or reduce the loans.

In the Teacher Loan Forgiveness Program, students are encouraged to join the teaching profession or to teach full-time for five consecutive years at an elementary or secondary level, or at schools or educational service agencies that serve low-income families to qualify.

While there are many criteria, this type of program is very helpful for those who meet the requirements.

Like the Teaching Loan Forgiveness Program, the Public Service Loan Forgiveness Program also encourages students to join and work full-time at public service jobs. With this program, students who make monthly payments will have their loans discharged after 10 years of full-time employment in public service. Students can qualify if they work with the federal, state, or local government, or other organizations designated as tax-exempt.

Men and women in uniform can get education benefits through the 9/11 GI Bill, and the different tuition assistance programs offered to them through the military. But despite this, many members of the military are still stuck with student loan debts. Fortunately, eligible military personnel can qualify for the Military Student Loan Forgiveness. Through different programs available to them, like the Public Service Loan Forgiveness or the National Defense Student Loan Discharge programs, men and women in the military can have their student loans reduced or completely discharged.

Students or veterans who are disabled and unemployable can have their student loans discharged under the Total Permanent Disability Discharge Program. While there are many requirements, the most important is to prove your disabilities and that you are unable to participate in any gainful activity because of physical or mental impairment.

Through certain civil organizations, students can volunteer their time and skills at schools, nonprofit agencies, faith-based groups, or private groups that provide humanitarian services or help eradicate social problems. Sometimes it can be volunteering within an underserved population. In exchange for volunteering, students who qualify can receive stipends and money toward their student loan payments or even a cancellation of certain loans. Well-known organizations such as AmeriCorps, Peace Corps, and Volunteers in Service to America (VISTA) offer volunteer opportunities in exchange for student loan perks. These organizations have their own criteria and differ on what they do. Check with each of them and see which one fits best with your inclinations and abilities.

Other career fields allow students to qualify for student loan forgiveness, especially those engaged in the healthcare industry, such as nurses or physicians, and those studying law. These industries have a staffing shortage and need people to work in underserved areas.

Aside from federal programs, other associations or organizations encourage and help students get a break from their debts if they enter such fields. Some states and local governments also provide help for students that need a financial break from their loans.

Many local governments, particularly those struggling with the problems of an aging population, are implementing programs in an effort to retain young adults after graduation. Students are offered the perks of student debt relief if they stay and work in the local communities. It's a win-win situation. Students can get their student debts paid off and the local government keeps its young workforce and boosts its economy.

Beyond assisting with their employees' college debt, many employers also help them by reimbursing all or a large portion of their student loans. Companies offer these benefits to attract and retain skilled workers. Find out the company's requirements; many require employees to work a certain number of years when their tuitions are reimbursed; otherwise, they have to pay it back.

Despite the availability of Student Loan Forgiveness Programs, many qualified students miss out on them, partly due to a lack of promotion for these programs.

Students in the quest for financial freedom should look into all possibilities. This includes checking with financial student offices, loan servicers, and organizations to see if you qualify for debt forgiveness; volunteering at an organization that helps discharge student loans; or seeking employment with a company that offers tuition reimbursement.

PART VII | College Savings Secrets

17

Uncovering the Hidden Expenses

We can't conclude our discussion on how to save and pay for college tuition without talking about the other costs related to college education.

Going to school doesn't only involve tuition, but other expenses like room, board, textbooks, transportation, and many more. Don't think you don't need to pay attention to those expenses because they may not be significant. To do so would be to make a huge mistake. I call them hidden expenses, and they add up quickly.

Zeroing Down on the Cost of Textbooks

You'll be surprised how much college textbooks cost, especially if you are getting them from your school bookstore. And it's a bad idea to get them there. I remember years ago, when I wasn't a very smart college shopper, I had to pay over $200 for one accounting book—and you never need just the one book!

Traditional textbooks are too expensive, can be out of date in a short time, and are sometimes too heavy to carry. While it may be convenient, don't rely on your school bookstore. Once you have your syllabus and know the books your professor needs you to get, find the book's ISBN and get your books somewhere cheaper.

The Internet is a vast marketplace where you can shop and buy your book(s) at better prices than in your bookstore. You can even compare the prices from different online bookstores, like Book.ly, Efollet, SwoopThat, Amazon, or Ebay, to see which site has the best deal.

Another option is to rent your textbooks. Why buy your books if you are only going to use them for one semester? That's an unnecessary expenditure. Instead, rent your book from your bookstore or an online marketplace like Chegg, known as the Netflix of textbooks, or from other places like BookRenter, Half. com, and AbeBooks. You can also rent your textbooks online and read them on a mobile device for less than the cost of the printed version.

Then again, why pay for expensive college textbooks when you can download them for free? OpenStax, an initiative from Rice University, is an alternative to expensive textbooks and provides free textbooks as well as other learning materials online. Quizlet also provides free study tools and applications.

If your textbook isn't available for free, many textbook publishers (Wiley, McGraw-Hill Education, CengageLearning, Pearson) have joined forces to create online e-textbooks at CourseSmart.com. There is a cost, but it is less expensive than purchasing traditional textbooks.

Maybe you have already taken a class that another classmate hasn't yet. Consider swapping books, so you don't each have to pay for them. If you don't have one to swap, you could borrow it. And if you buy your book, remember that when you are done with it, you can sell it back to your bookstore, or online.

If you want or need a traditional printed book, consider buying a used book. An international edition that might have negligible differences in the text might also be a cheaper option.

Certain libraries carry textbooks, which you can check out for free. Some libraries are even going digital, such as the Florida Polytechnic University library, which has almost 135,000 e-books but no printed books at all.

Other College Expenses

Don't go on a shopping spree for the "recommended list of things to buy" your college sent you. Instead, look for alternatives. If you have a roommate and know his or her contact information, you could coordinate purchases with that person in advance. No need to buy that minifridge if he or she has one already. In return, you could buy the microwave. Buy used items from places like Goodwill or shop at discount stores to save money.

There is no need to bring your cool car to college only to have it sit in the parking lot for days and accrue expensive parking rates, especially at urban colleges. Leave it home unless you are planning to use it very often. Insurance and maintenance are also considerable expenses. To save money, use bicycles or public transportation. Use car-sharing services like Zipcar or U Car to get around if you really need to drive.

Joining certain clubs on campus isn't cheap. Joining a fraternity or sorority, for example, can easily cost a student $3,500. Be creative and consider getting scholarships that will cover dues and look into the possibility of renting your gowns and clothes.

Remember that you are a student, even if your school looks like a fancy hotel. Schools can offer students great packages on services such as laundry and running errands for a fee. While the convenience may be tempting, choose to save your money by doing those errands and laundry yourself.

Why pay for an expensive meal plan if you may not use it? Many students pay for but barely use their meal plans. Instead, they spend more money to order fast food or eat from restaurants. It's like paying twice for food!

Schools may offer what appears to be a great deal with a bundle for all the football and basketball games. Ask yourself if you will really watch those games. If you won't, then it's not worth it.

College should be fun! I don't disagree. But while having fun, you need to keep in mind that you can't spend all your money on booze, food or other related "fun" items. Be a responsible spender and prioritize where your money goes.

Saving money in college requires good money management skills. But by reducing and eliminating these hidden costs, students can save a lot of money.

18

Don't Settle for Being a Cool Student, Be Cool with Money

The Importance of Financial Literacy Education

Financial literacy helps people better manage money or become financially capable. It's a necessary skill for college students to acquire, so they can make wise financial decisions while in school or after school.

The recent financial crisis was an eye-opener that highlights the importance of financial education in general but, more importantly, for young people starting out in life. And since one of the reasons for going to college is to have higher incomes, financial literacy is that much more important.

While some schools have made financial education a requirement, others offer it as an elective, or implement programs where students can go for counseling and to learn money management skills. But not all schools teach personal finance. There is still a lot to do to raise awareness of the importance of good money management skills and to encourage students to take interest in such a valuable subject. A college student might take many classes with no practical application to his or her life. But when it comes to money skills, we all need them. They have a direct impact on the lives of students. Money management is a life skill. We all use it all the time.

While I can't cover all the necessary topics about personal finance here, I believe college students should be knowledgeable on how to budget, shop smart, save, manage debts, and be aware of identity theft.

You Can't Go Wrong with Budgeting

Students may receive money from different sources, like family, scholarships, endowments from grants, or earnings from working part-time. They spend money on tuition, rent, food, books, and other items. Receiving, earning, and spending money requires tracking and planning and budgeting.

Budgeting, or a spending plan, is essential to money management. It's the foundation of a responsible fiscal approach and allows students to know how much money comes in and to control how much money goes out.

A budget has two components: income and expenses. Income is money earned from wages, salaries, or alimony or interest. For students, it's money from scholarships, grants, and student loans. Expenses are divided into four categories:

- Fixed Expenses: the same almost every month. These are expenses that don't change, like rent, car payments, tuition, etc.

- Variable Expenses: they change every month, like cost of food, transportation, some utilities, etc.

- Periodic Expenses: occurring once in a while, like insurance premiums, start of semester materials, etc.

- Discretionary Expenses: unnecessary and unneeded. Something people can do without, like going out, movies, shopping, etc.

When budgeting, keep in mind that your expenses should not exceed your income, and if that always happens, look at your expenses to see what you can cut down on.

Allocating a specific amount to specific expenses helps. If you allocate $70 for entertainment expenses, and if that money is gone before the end of the month, then you shouldn't go out any longer. Don't take funds allocated to another category.

As incomes change, it's a good idea to revisit your budget frequently, every month or few months. Make adjustments based on different events that affect your financial life.

Make Saving a Priority

While in college, you probably wouldn't have enough money left over after your expenses to put money into savings. But saving money doesn't just mean putting money aside. It also means being a responsible spender and having a good attitude when it comes to money.

Students should know the difference between "wants" and "needs." It's easy to become an impulsive buyer. But those gadgets and other little things can wait. Before making those purchases, always ask yourself: Do I need it? Sleep on it if you have to. By giving it a second (and third and fourth) thought, and weighing your options, even students can resist pure impulse buys and save money.

Don't just shop, shop smart. Compare prices and see where you can get things at the best price. Convenience stores like the one at your campus may be pricier. Buy things like your toiletries in bulk. Go in with your family, friends, or dorm mates for bulk purchases. You can save money. Many retail stores give students discounts. Always ask for one. Try to never have to pay full price.

If you save money on purchases, you can have something left over at the end of the month. That can go into a savings account, to be accumulated and then invested.

Be Great at Debt Management

Credit card companies can no longer hand credit cards to students like they used to do in the past, but it doesn't mean that students don't have credit cards. Here are some tips to manage credit cards:

- Read and understand the terms of your credit cards.

- Show that you are a responsible cardholder by paying your card on time every month.

- Don't just pay the minimum payment, otherwise your payment isn't going toward your principal. Pay more than the minimum or pay the full amount.

- Avoid cash advances on your credit card or using courtesy checks the card issuer sends in the mail. They are synonymous with high interest.

- Don't charge everything on your credit card. Small items add up and can amount to a bigger balance.

- Use your credit card to build credit on things you can afford to buy, then pay off the balance right away.

In addition to credit cards, students might have to deal with their student loans, which we already discussed in chapter 15, so extra care should be taken. Don't let debts pile up.

By properly managing their credit card and student loan debts, students will be able to have a good credit score and afford bigger purchases at lower interest rates.

Be on Guard against Identity Theft

Students are particularly vulnerable to identity theft— the use of someone else's identity to obtain benefits or to commit crimes. By sharing a room, using computers at the school libraries, or visiting certain sites, students' personal information can be in jeopardy.

Identity theft is a major threat and a very scary situation with painful consequences. Lately, big retail stores like Target, Nordstrom, and Home Depot and even UPS and some financial institutions have had their accounts hacked into, exposing consumers' personal information.

Apply these tips to avoid being victimized by identity theft:

- Protect your personal information. Don't leave around documents that contain information such as your Social Security number, birthdate, etc., even if you trust your roommate.

- Avoid making purchases from websites you don't know. Only make transactions with trusted sites.

- Never open attachments from junk emails.

- Always have strong passwords mixed with letters, numbers, and characters, and change them often.

- Browse from a secured network.

- Do not check your bank account or access sites with your personal information on public computers.

- Get your credit report often.

Put Technology on Your Side

Since we live in the digital age, students can use technology to shop, budget, and save money. There are even smartphone apps that students can use while shopping, like price comparison apps, to save or monitor their money. From a tap on their smartphone, they can check their bank account, set up alerts once a purchase is made, or download the popular budgeting app from mint.com.

The End Is the Beginning

You made it. Congratulations! You have come to the end of *Screw College Debt*. I want to thank you for taking the time to read this guide that not only explains some of our higher education challenges, but also provides tips, ideas, and resources on how to save and pay for college.

If you're heading to college, I applaud you. You have just taken the most important step on your path to college success.

If you're in college, this is your opportunity to plan strategically, avoid hidden expenses and debt, and maximize the return of your investment.

If you have already come out of college buried under a load of debt, there may be options for you from refinancing or debt forgiveness, to name just two. Check them out!

If you are a parent, it can be daunting and stressful to think and plan for higher education. Focus on how you can help and support your student through the process, perhaps by scholarship searches or funding a 529 plan. Remember: Don't jeopardize your retirement goals to fund your child's education.

My hope is that *Screw College Debt* will contribute to helping thousands of people plan better for college—and reduce or avoid college debt. The end of this book is the beginning of your opportunity. Now that you have finished reading the book, it's your turn to come up with your action plans for avoiding college debt. I have provided you with tips and thought-provoking questions to guide you in the process. I encourage you to use the following pages to write down your own plans.

My Action Plans

_____

_____

_____

_____

_____

_____

_____

_____

_____

_____

_____

_____

My Action Plans

_____

_____

_____

_____

_____

_____

_____

_____

_____

_____

_____

_____

100-at-a-Glance Tips on How to Avoid and Pay for College Debt

1. Know your debts before owing them.
2. Understand the financial aid process.
3. Know your financial players.
4. Choose your academic major carefully.
5. Make the right choice for school.
6. Invest in a 529 College Savings Plan.
7. Maximize retirement funding before funding your child's 529 plan.
8. Students should borrow first; then parents borrow, if needed.
9. Seek scholarships, even smaller ones.
10. Favor federal loans over private loans.
11. Financial aid doesn't always mean "free money!"
12. Don't buy everything with your student loan money.
13. Be ahead of the game in the college planning process.
14. Assess if you will have a return on your investment.
15. Find value in your education.
16. Stay on top of repayment.
17. Avoid default on student loans.
18. Know your loan servicers.
19. Know the fees and expenses that come with your college loans.
20. Start saving earlier for college.
21. Have a savings goal when saving for college.
22. Ask a relative to help with college savings programs.
23. Pay interest on your loans while still in school.

24.   Try community college.

25.   Research your school before attending.

26.   Live below your means while in college.

27.   Have a plan in mind before heading to college.

28.   Develop a budget.

29.   Maximize your financial aid.

30.   Consider working while in school.

31.   Negotiate payments with lenders.

32.   Pay more than the minimum payments.

33.   Focus on paying your debts with higher interest rates first.

34.   Look for real tuition deals.

35.   Consider the Massive Open Online Courses (MOOCs).

36.   Use college savings tools.

37.   Understand and compare college savings investment options.

38.   Don't ignore your student loans.

39.   Student loans aren't dischargeable under bankruptcy.

40.   Hunt for loan forgiveness programs.

41.   Know your grace period.

42.   Know the types of loans you have.

43.   Choose the right student loan repayment plans.

44.   Look overseas for tuition deals.

45.   Seek alternative lenders.

46.   Pay attention to the fine print when signing documents.

47.   Enroll in automatic payment plans.

48.   Take advantage of tax credits.

49.   Avoid cosigning for student loans.

50.   Explore careers before choosing your major.

51. Don't assume you won't qualify for financial aid.

52. Pick schools that want you.

53. Don't wait until the last minute to apply for financial aid.

54. Negotiate your financial award.

55. Take college classes while in high school.

56. Avoid defaulting on your loans.

57. As last resort, check if deferment or forbearance applies to you.

58. Build a college support team.

59. Be an informed consumer.

60. Prepare your applications carefully and respect deadlines.

61. Start searching early for scholarships.

62. Get great results for ACT and SAT.

63. Pay your debts as soon as possible.

64. Seek a college with free tuition.

65. Work at college to get discounts on tuition.

66. Consider online classes.

67. Take more credits per term.

68. Save money on textbooks.

69. Consider alternative housing.

70. Use student discounts.

71. Stay on top of your repayment obligation.

72. Only borrow what you need.

73. Become an entrepreneur.

74. Consider colleges that guarantee an education in four years.

75. Don't overuse forbearance and deferment.

76. Prioritize your student loan debts.

77. Keep track of your loans.

78. Avoid private loans.

79.   Choose more than one school.

80.   Apply for as many scholarships as you can.

81.   Protect your personal information while living on campus.

82.   Get involved in college.

83.   Attend your industry conference while in school.

84.   Network with professionals in your field.

85.   Keep your grades up.

86.   Consider trade schools.

87.   Know why you are going to college.

88.   Know how much college will cost today and in the future.

89.   Be a responsible student while in college.

90.   Monetize by selling your skills.

91.   Manage your time, and make priorities.

92.   Be aware of scholarship scams.

93.   Take courses that will help you succeed.

94.   Attend college and financial aid fairs.

95.   Get an internship while in college.

96.   Be financially educated.

97.   Complete your degree in three years.

98.   Seek out unusual scholarships.

99.   Know the rules of student loan borrowing.

100. Don't major in debt.

Discussion Questions

1. Is college education worth racking up student debt?

2. Is college debt a good debt or bad debt?

3. How are tuition costs rising at most colleges and universities?

4. Why do students drop out of college?

5. Will college debt create the next financial crisis?

6. Why are people against higher education?

7. What are the values of colleges and universities in our communities?

8. Why do people go to college?

9. What is financial aid?

10. What are the differences between private and federal loans?

11. What are the benefits of federal loans?

12. Why are students defaulting on their loans?

13. What are the best ways to pay for college?

14. What is the dark side of student loans?

15. Is a college education necessary to be successful?

16. Why don't students graduate on time?

17. How can college debt be managed?

18. What is income-based payment?

19. How are student loans playing a role in bankruptcy?

20. How can student loans threaten Social Security benefits?

21. Why are graduates stressed over their loans and debts?

22. What are 529 plans?

23. Will massive open online courses replace traditional schools?

24. Online versus traditional degree, which one is better?

25. How can you pay for college on your own?

26. How can you find cheaper loans for colleges?

27. How to plan for college?

28. How to choose your school?

29. How to choose the right college investment plans?

30. What is financial aid?

31. What are the techniques to score scholarships?

32. Why shouldn't you cosign a college loan?

33. What are the college repayment plans?

34. Why is it important to know the details of your loans?

35. Does the price tag of a school matter?

36. What is an American Opportunity Tax?

37. Why is it important to take college courses while in high school?

38. Who qualifies for student loan forgiveness programs?

39. Who is eligible to take out federal student loans?

40. What is a grace period?

41. Is it possible to discharge student loans under bankruptcy?

42. What is the difference between default and delinquency?

43. How does a school net price calculator work?

44. How can you avoid default on loans?

45. What happens to my credit rating when a loan is defaulted?

46. How can I save money while in college?

47. How can I fund my college education?

48. Why is going to college a personal choice?

49. Why is it important to have goal(s) when going to college?

50. How can I find value in higher education?

Recommended Sources

Chany, Kalman. *Paying for College Without Going Broke.* Princeton Review, 2013.

Cruze, Rachel. *The Graduate's Survival Guide* (Book & DVD). Lampo Press, 2011.

Ellis, Kristina. *Confessions of a Scholarship Winner: The Secret That Helped Me Win $500,000 in Free Money for College—How You Can Too!* Worthy Publishing, 2013.

Jacobs, Lynn F. and Hyman, Jeremy S. *The Secrets of College Success.* Jossey-Bass, 2010.

Kantrowitz, Mark and Levy, David. *Filing the FAFSA: The Edvisors Guide to Completing the Free Application for Federal Student Aid.* Edvisors Network, Inc., 2014.

Stephens, Dale J. *Hacking Your Education: Ditch the Lectures, Save Ten of Thousands, and Learn More Than Your Peers Ever Will.* Perigee Trade, 2013.

Recommended Documentary

Rossi, Andrew, Writer/Director. *The Ivory Tower*. Participant Media, 2014. Distributed by Samuel Goldwyn Films.

Valuable Websites

College News, Data & Research

College board.org
Collegedata.com
Deltacostproject.org
Ed.gov
Ny.frb.org
Projectonstudentdebt.org
Treasury.gov
USNews.com

College Planning

Chegg.com
Edvisors.com
Fafsa.ed.gov
Finaid.org
Nerdwallet.com
Simpletuition.com
Studentaid.ed.gov
TheCollegeSolution.com
Unigo.com

College Debt Management

Cappex.com
Consumerfinance.gov
Finaid.org
Sofi.com
Studentloans.gov

Scholarships

FastWeb.com
Scholarships.com
Scholarships101.com
    (www.cibc.com/ca/student-life/paying-for-education/
    financial-aid/scholarships-101.html)
Scholarshipmonkey.com
Supercollege.com
Zinch.com

Textbooks

Aboutfollettebooks.com
Amazon.com
Campusbookrentals.com
Campusbooks.com
Half.com (www.half.ebay.com/)

Savings

Bigfuture.collegebaord.org

CollegeSavings.org

Finra.org

Nest529Direct.com

Savingsforcollege.com

UPromise.com

Vanguard529CollegePlan.com
(personal.vanguard.com/us/whatweoffer/college/
vanguard529)

Online Education

Coursera.org

Edx.org

KhanAcademy.org

Udacity.com

Udemy.com

WGU.edu

Acknowledgments

Writing this book is truly a testament to teamwork and dedication. This project would not have been possible without the contributions of the many individuals who allowed me to interview them, shared their stories, and provided me with valuable information.

First, I am grateful to all the leaders in their respective fields who reviewed and honored *Screw College Debt* with endorsements.

Thanks to the editors: Joanna Paula Cailas; Robin Dorman and Ann Maynard at Command +Z Content. Special thanks to Sandra Wendel for improving the quality of this book.

It's a great pleasure to be working with April Bailey at Bailey Creative. She approaches every project with an innovative mindset. Thank you for providing me with guidance from the start to the finish of this project.

To Lisa Pelto and her team at Concierge Marketing, thank you for bringing this project to life.

I have had the privilege to know and work with Lynn McCormick for many years. Thank you and your team at Proforma for always integrating my ideas into real products that help promote my work.

To my great friend Modu Seye, founder of Moduvated, your motivation is contagious. Thank you for your feedback and for continuing to inspire me.

To my friend John Ekeh, founder at Ekeh law firm, thank you for your friendship and generosity in helping others.

I will always be grateful to the Slattery family for their generosity and guidance.

To Richard Kissi and Angelo Afanou, thanks for assisting, guiding, and motivating me every step along the way during the course of this project.

I owe thanks to the following people who either supported, encouraged, or inspired me in many ways: Melissa Seitelbach Beagley, Gena Schriver, Gerald Vossah, Tracy Russell, Sarah Wernimont, Zozo Samani, and Ryan & Amanda Medinger, Jean Amouzou, Chris Snyder & Angela Brant.

A big thank you to my family, including my cousins Benito, Andy, Dela; my sisters Viviane, Kafui, and Dominique; my parents, Lydia and Antoine; and, most importantly, my wife, Gina, and my greatest gift, my daughter Elizabeth Kay.

Lastly, but not the least, YOU, reading this book. I want to thank you for your support.

Notes

Introduction

1. "Quarterly Report on Household Debt & Credit," Federal Reserve Bank of New York, May 2014.

2. Friedman, Dan. "Americans Owe $1.2 Trillion in Student Loans, Surpassing Credit Card and Auto Loan Debt Totals." *New York Daily News*, May 17, 2014, http://www.nydailynews.com/news/national/americans-owe-1-2-trillion-student-loans-article-1.1796606.

Chapter 1 — Tuition Marathon

1. "College Spending in a Turbulent Decade." Delta Cost Project 2000–2010

2. "Degrees of Difficulty." *Time*, October 2012

3. "The Debt Crisis In Higher Education," *Time*, October 2012.

4. "Cost of College Degree in U.S. Soars 12 Fold," *Bloomberg*, August 15, 2012, http://www.bloomberg.com/news/2012-08-15/cost-of-college-degree-in-u-s-soars-12-fold-chart-of-the-day.html.

5. "UNL Tuition Hikes Outpacing Inflation," *Omaha World-Herald*. June 3, 2012.

6. "Trends in College Pricing 2012," *The College Board*, http://trends.collegeboard.org/sites/default/files/college-pricing-2012-full-report_0.pdf.

7. "Open Doors 2012: International Student Enrollment Increases by Nearly 6%," *ICEF Monitor*, November 12, 2012, http://monitor.icef.com/2012/11/open-doors-2012-international-student-enrolment-increases-by-nearly-6-percent/.

8. "Get Football Out of Our Universities," *Forbes*, February 15, 2011, http://www.forbes.com/sites/sciencebiz/2011/02/15/get-football-out-of-our-universities/.

9. "Executive Compensation at Public Colleges," *The Chronicle of Higher Education*, May 20, 2012, http://chronicle.com/article/What-Public-College-Presidents/131912/?sid=at&utm_source=at&utm_medium=en.

10. "Administrative Bloat at American Universities: The Real Reason for High Costs in Higher Education," *Goldwater Institute*, August 17, 2010, http://goldwaterinstitute.org/article/administrative-bloat-american-universities-real-reason-high-costs-higher-education.

Chapter 2 — Lack of College Planning

1. "Tuition Inflation," *FinAid: The Smart Guide to Financial Aid*, http://www.finaid.org/savings/tuition-inflation.phtml.

2. "Where and Who the College Graduates Are," *The Chronicle of Higher Education*, February 24, 2013, https://chronicle.com/article/WhereWho-the-College/137551/?key=HTlyJ1c7NSQTMHBqMjZCYzcDOidrYkJ0aycYOS5xbllUFw%3D%3D#notes.

3.   "The Debt-Free College Degree," *Bloomberg Businessweek*, September 6, 2012, http://www.businessweek.com/ articles/2012-09-06/the-debt-free-college-degree.

4.   Midland University's Four-Year Graduation Guarantee, http:// www.midlandu.edu/guarantee.

5.   "College Costs 2014: Undergraduate Student Borrowing Decreases as Economy Heals, Enrollment Shifts," *International Business Times*, November 13, 2014, http://www.ibtimes. com/college-costs-2014-undergraduate-student-borrowing-decreases-economy-heals-enrollment-1723383.

Chapter 6 — Finding Value in Higher Education

1.   "Is College Worth It? Clearly, New Data Say," *New York Times*, May 27, 2014, http://www.nytimes.com/2014/05/27/upshot/is-college-worth-it-clearly-new-data-say.html?abt=0002&abg=1.

2.   U.S. Department of Labor Employment Projections, http:// www.bls.gov/emp/ep_chart_001.htm.

Chapter 7 — Is College for You?

1.   "Google Cares Less about SAT Scores and GPA because They Have Better Hiring Data," *Business Insider*, April 23, 2013, http://www.businessinsider.com/data-in-the-workplace-2013-4.

2.   "It Takes More than a Major: Employer Priorities for College Learning and Student Success: Overview for Key Findings," Association of American Colleges and Universities, https://www.aacu.org/leap/presidentstrust/ compact/2013SurveySummary.

3.   "Finessing Financial Aid," *CNN Money*, April 2012. cnnmoney.com.

4.   "College Salary Report," *Pay Scale*, http://www.payscale.com/college-salary-report.

Chapter 8 — Be in the Know

1.   "Beyond Financial Aid," *FinAid: The Smart Guide to Financial Aid*, http://www.finaid.org/beyond/.

2.   "Know Before You Own: Student Loans Project," CFPB (Consumer Financial Protections Bureau), http://www.consumerfinance.gov/students/knowbeforeyouowe/.

Chapter 9 — Community Colleges Still Win

1.   "Where Value Meets Values: The Economic Impact of Community Colleges, Analysis of the Economic Impact & Return on Investment of Education," American Association of Community Colleges, February 2014.

Chapter 10 — Investing in a College Education

1.   Financial Student Aid Main Site, www.federalStudentAid.ed.gov.

2.   http://www.KnowHow2GoIllinois.org.

3.   "Smart Saving for College—Better Buy Degrees," FINRA (Financial Industry Regulatory Authority), http://www.finra.org/Investors/SmartInvesting/SmartSavingForCollege/.

Chapter 11 — The Beauty of Scholarships

1.   Fastweb Scholarship Database, http://www.fastweb.com/college-scholarships.

2. "Crowd Fund a Scholarship," *Kiplinger Personal Finance Magazine*, June 2012.

3. "Scholarship Money for Fallen Soldier's Kids," *CNN Money*, April 2012, cnn.money.com.

4. Financial Student Aid Main Site, http://www.finaid.org/scholarships/average.phtml.

5. "Scholarship Scams," *The Costco Connection*, September 2013.

Chapter 12 — Alternative Ways to Pay for College

1. "Steven A. Schwarzman," *Blackstone Group*, http://www.blackstone.com/the-firm/overview/our-people/stephen-a-schwarzman.

2. "Find Cheap(er) Loans for College," *CNN Money*, April 2012, cnnmoney.com.

3. "Let Your Fellow Harvard Grads Pay for That MBA," *Bloomberg Businessweek*, July 9-15, 2012.

Chapter 13 — Savings through Digital Education

1. "Tuition and Financial Aid," Western Governors University, http://www.wgu.edu/tuition_financial_aid/overview.

Chapter 14 — Higher Education on the Cheap

1. "Make a Digital Degree Pay Off," *Money,* June 2011.

2. "The University of Disruption," *Forbes*, June 2012.

3. "Will MOOCs Help You Open Career Doors?" *Boston Globe*, October 6, 2013, http://www.bostonglobe.com/business/2013/10/05/will-mooc-help-you-open-career-doors/pmjHbLCghsH0lEbulWC9VL/story.html.

Chapter 15 — Loan Repayment Plans

1. Federal Student Aid, https://studentaid.ed.gov.

2. "Getting Rid of the College Loan Repo Man," *Washington Monthly*, October–December 2012.

Chapter 16 — Student Debt Forgiveness Programs

1. "Forgiveness, Cancellation, and Discharge," Federal Student Aid, https://studentaid.ed.gov/repay-loans/forgiveness-cancellation.

About the Author

Marco LeRoc is an entrepreneur and founder of Marco LeRoc & Co., an organization that inspires millennials to succeed in the areas of personal finance and personal development. Marco is a leader and a go-getter, committed to supporting his generation.

He is a Certified Educator in Personal Finance. As a coach, Marco supports and encourages young adults to promote themselves so they can achieve their most significant financial and personal goals, which was the theme of his first book, Cash In with Your Money: Tools for a Better Financial Life.

A native of the West African country of Togo, Marco came to the United States in 2004. He earned his college degree in accounting at Metropolitan Community College and Bellevue University debt-free and loves to share with students and parents tips on how to succeed in college and avoid college debt. This book is the result of his experience and expertise.

As an international speaker, Marco is a sought-after expert on money issues and personal development matters around the world. He frequently speaks to high school, college, and association audiences, addressing a range of topics including confidence, failure, positive thinking, financial literacy, budgeting, savings, investing, identity theft, and college planning.

An avid volunteer, Marco serves as the Co-President of the local Junior Chamber International and sits on the board of the

Hidden Talent Foundation, as well as volunteers with a variety of other organizations. Marco is a member of the Financial Planning Association and the Nebraska Council on Economic Education.

Marco and his wife, Eugenia, and their daughter, Elizabeth, make their home in Omaha, Nebraska.

Connect with Marco LeRoc on:

Facebook
Twitter
LinkedIn
MarcoLeRoc.com

Also by Marco LeRoc

Cash in with Your Money: Tools for a Better Financial Life
ISBN: 978-0-9903612-1-3
Price: $14.95

40208001R00112

Made in the USA
Charleston, SC
30 March 2015